Praise for the Innovative Leadership Workbook for Nonprofit Executives

As someone charged with the stewardship of a social benefit organization, the challenge is always there to find tools to help navigate what sometimes are obscure paths to create change. We find ourselves adrift without a comprehensible map to guide us. The workbook is an insightful tool that serves not only as a compass, but as a catalyst to embrace self-development as a lifetime process and leadership as lifelong learning.

Elisa Sabatini, Executive Director, Via International

The *Innovative Leadership Workbook for Nonprofit Executives* lays out a process for transformation, and includes a discussion of organizational culture, an exploration of and tools for improving personal and professional leadership style, and an in-depth description of the role of the nonprofit CEO. This is a must-read for senior leadership staff and the boards they serve.

John Hrusovsky, Partner QSI, former CEO, GroundWork group

The development process and tools laid out in the *Innovative Leadership Workbook for Nonprofit Executives* provide a clear direction for nonprofit leaders to strengthen and increase their skills. Particularly during times of funding cuts—but increased needs—our leaders need to invest in their own skills to ensure they can optimally deliver for their agencies.

Sidney R. Hargro, Executive Director, Community Foundation of South Jersey

The *Innovative Leadership Workbook for Nonprofit Executives* offers an honest development journey of a leader in a community-based nonprofit. Her insightful story provides an example of how an individual—sharing power with colleagues and stakeholders as part of an organization—can change a community. Use this workbook to supercharge the impact you make by continuing to develop your leadership skills.

Philip Cass, Ph.D., Chief Executive Officer, Columbus Medical Association and Affiliates

The *Innovative Leadership Workbook for Nonprofit Executives* provides valuable insight and information for nonprofit executives. The case study offers a beautiful example of the personal development journey of an experienced nonprofit executive. The workbook is a must have for your personal development and for that of your team. Skillfully written and well designed, the workbook leads readers on a path toward personal and professional growth and increased effectiveness.

Paul Pyrz, President, LeaderShape

I know the *Innovative Leadership Workbook for Nonprofit Executives* will become a favorite tool for nonprofit thought and action leaders for its practical, no-nonsense and comprehensive approach to building effective and compassionate leadership skills and attitudes during this period when nonprofit outcomes and results are more important than ever for our communities.

Robert A. Kulinski, President, United Way of Summit County

Holding the reins of a community-based nonprofit is a challenge in the best of times and much more difficult in challenging times. The *Innovative Leadership Workbook for Nonprofit Executives* offers steps for improving your own leadership style and transforming your organization. The "fly on the wall" access as one CEO figures out her path forward reminds us that we are not alone. Buy it, implement its wisdom, and get ready to soar!

Natasha Spears, Executive Director, Boys & Girls Club of Dayton

■■■■■■■

There are compelling reasons for re-evaluating our notions about leadership and innovation. The landscape for leadership has changed. The stakes are higher and the demands for innovation never have been so great to solve our most pressing problems. The *Innovative Leadership Workbook for Nonprofit Executives* is a response to these realities. It provides the opportunity and an open invitation to take a good look at yourself as a leader through an exploration of six stages of leadership development that are essential for new levels of effectiveness, contribution, and results. What I like most about the book is its thoughtful, practical, step-by-step approach to re-evaluating and reinventing how you lead. It is one of those books that become a ready-reference for your personal ongoing leadership journey of renewal and growth.

Debbe Kennedy, Founder, President and CEO, Global Dialogue Center and Leadership Solutions Companies, Author of Putting Our Differences to Work: The Fastest Way to Innovation, Leadership, and High Performance

■■■■■■■

The seismic shifts in both the economy and the nonprofit sector over the last decade require all leaders to reassess how they lead and manage towards accomplishment of mission. Robbins and Metcalf have taken both their successful and not-so-successful experiences, and used them as valuable teaching tools for the rest of us. The *Innovative Leadership Workbook for Nonprofit Executives* is a guide that each board member and leadership staff should go through as part of leadership development. It forces each leader to create a compelling vision that motivates real change, and gives them the tools and processes to realize that change.

John R. Miller, Regional Vice President, Boys & Girls Clubs of America

■■■■■■■

Authors Metcalf and Robbins draw upon their own experiences and research to cast a fresh, insightful eye upon what it takes to innovatively lead a nonprofit organization in a quickly changing world. This is a must-have manual for any nonprofit leader, board member, or individual aspiring to become an organizational leader. Metcalf and Robbins write in a lively style, pose lots of compelling questions, and offer plenty of practical examples to illustrate their points. Readers will find the module-style of this workbook to be enormously useful—boards can use modules independently to enhance strategic planning sessions, while leaders can work sequentially through the modules to maximize personal growth. Metcalf and Robbins not only force us to ask important and difficult questions of our own leadership styles, but challenge us to create a dramatically more productive future for our organizations.

Megan Kilgore, Founder and Board President, Ohio Women in Public Finance

INNOVATIVE LEADERSHIP WORKBOOK FOR NONPROFIT EXECUTIVES

Field-Tested Processes and Worksheets for Innovating Leadership, Creating Sustainability, and Transforming Organizations

MAUREEN METCALF | DANI A. ROBBINS

WORKBOOK SERIES EDITOR: MARK PALMER

First Published by
Integral Publishers
1418 N. Jefferson Ave.
Tucson, AZ 85712

Published in the United States with printing and
distribution in the United Kingdom, Australia, and
the European Union.

ISBN: 978-1-4675-2278-6

First Printing July 2012

Cover Design, Graphics and Layout by
Creative Spot - www.creativespot.com

Acknowledgments

Contributing Authors: Belinda Gore, Ph.D. and Mark Palmer

The theoretical giants on whose hard work we built the Innovative Leadership Fieldbook model: Terri O'Fallon, Ph.D., Susanne Cook-Greuter, Ph.D., Hilke Richmer, Ed.D., Roxanne Howe-Murphy, Ed.D., Peter Senge, Ph.D., Cindy Wigglesworth, M.A., and Ken Wilber, M.A., who not only shared their theories, but whose ongoing guidance and encouragement helped us create a solid framework that is comprehensive and theoretically grounded.

Our friends and colleagues who served as constant cheerleaders and occasional editors, listened to our stories and dreams about the book, and helped us make it come to fruition.

Our teachers, trainers, and mentors, who taught us how to lead—and when to follow.

Our clients who participated as case studies, as well as MBA students who gave feedback on the Fieldbook by virtue of doing graduate work that served as the foundation for this workbook.

Our families who inspired us to be thoughtful and dedicated to our work, and to contribute to the world in a meaningful way.

Our publisher and friend, Russ Volckmann, Ph.D.

Graphic design and layout firm Creative Spot, copy editor Sara Phelps, as well as editors, reviewers, endorsers, thought partners, and countless others who spent untold hours making this possible.

Table of Contents

INNOVATIVE LEADERSHIP

Leadership and innovation are two of the most compelling topics in business today. Yet despite the volume of resources exploring both topics, most approaches provide directional solutions that are merely anecdotal and lack sufficient information to actually allow leaders to make measurable change. We know that leadership plays a critical role in an organization's long-term success, and that innovation has become a strategic necessity in today's business environment. In short, both leadership and innovation have a greater impact today than ever before. Technology and increased access to information continue to accentuate their roles, yet organizations are often too overrun with change to handle the torrent of emerging demands.

Still, ensuing questions on how to lead and where to innovate remain puzzlingly philosophical: What is the role of leadership in a time of looming uncertainty? How will organizations innovate to overcome challenges that are largely unprecedented? In a new climate of business, what is the formula for creating success in both areas?

This workbook is designed to help answer those questions and help you to perform the critical self-evaluation needed to refine and innovate your own leadership skills. It is fundamentally about leadership, yet equally an account of applying innovation. Leadership needs innovation the way innovation demands leadership, and by marrying the two, you can improve your capacity for growth and improved effectiveness.

This workbook explores a number of approaches to elaborate on both areas, not just conceptually, but tangibly, by providing exercises designed to enhance your leadership skills. Most importantly, any meaningful advancement concerning both must originate from you. In other words, becoming a better leader and optimizing innovation jointly hinge on your ability to authentically examine your own inner makeup, which will allow you to make real change.

At the same time, you must diligently address some challenging limitations. Despite their collective value, many conventional applications of leadership and innovation have often proven elusive and even problematic in real-world scenarios. For example, if the leadership team of a struggling organization drives initiatives that focus solely on making innovative changes to incentives, products, and services, without also advancing strategic purpose, culture, and team cohesiveness, they will ultimately miss the greater potential to create a meaningful turn-around in the organization. Productivity and system improvements are undoubtedly critical, but how employees make sense of their work experience is equally vital to team engagement and commitment. Innovating products and improving functionality—without also creating a better team environment or a more supportive organizational culture—often appears to pay off in the short term, yet produces lopsided decision-making and shortsighted leadership that have lasting adverse consequences.

Knowing that the future of organizations is irrevocably tied to a world of erratic change, we can no longer afford to improve our systems and offerings without equally advancing our leadership capacity. Leadership empathy and the ability to inspire cultural alignment, along with other important leadership activities, will make a significant impact on your organization and must be implemented as shrewdly as strategic planning.

Combining leadership with innovation, then, requires you to transform the way you perceive yourself, others, and your business. By vigorously looking into your own experience, including motivations, inclinations, interpersonal skills, and proficiencies, you can optimize your effectiveness in the current dynamic environment. Through deep examination and reflection, you learn to balance the hard skills you have acquired with meaningful introspection, all the while setting the stage for further growth. In essence, you discover how to strategically and tactically innovate leadership the same way you innovate in other aspects of your business.

Marrying Innovation and Leadership

Let's explore innovating leadership in a more tangible way by defining it in practical terms. This, of course, begs the obvious question: *what does innovating leadership really mean?*

It is important to first understand each topic beyond its more conventional meaning. For example, most definitions of leadership alone are almost exclusively fashioned around emulating certain kinds of behaviors: leader X did "this" to achieve success, and leader Y did "that" to enhance organizational performance.

Even if initially useful, such approaches are still, essentially, formulas for *imitating leadership*, and are therefore likely ineffectual over the long term. Innovating leadership cannot be applied as a monolithic theory, or as simple prescriptive guidance. It must take place through your own intelligence and stem from your own unique sensibilities.

In order to enhance this unique awareness process you will need a greater foundational basis from which to explore both topics, which means talking about them in a different context entirely.

Let's start by straightforwardly defining leadership:

> **Leadership is a process of influencing people strategically and tactically, affecting change in intentions, actions, culture, and systems.**

Within this context, and above all else, leadership involves a ***process of influence***: strategic influence to inspire vision and direction; tactical influence to guide functional execution.

Leadership influences individual intentions and cultural norms by inspiring purpose and alignment. It equally influences an individual's actions and organizational efficiencies through tactical decisions.

Innovation, as an extension of leadership, refers to the novel ways in which we advance that influence personally, behaviorally, culturally, and systematically throughout the organization.

> **Innovation is a novel advancement that influences organizations: personally, behaviorally, culturally, and systematically.**

Notice here that in addition to linking the relationship of leadership to innovation, we're also relating to them as an essential part of our individual experience. Just as with leadership and innovation, the way you uniquely experience and influence the world is defined through a mutual interplay of personal, behavioral, cultural, and systematic events. These same core dimensions that ground leadership and innovation also provide a context and mirror for *your total experience* in any given moment or on any given occasion.

Optimally then, leadership is influencing through an explicit balancing of those core dimensions. Innovation naturally follows as a creative advancement of this basic alignment. In our experience, leadership and innovation are innately connected and share a deep commonality.

Therefore, marrying leadership with innovation allows you to ground and articulate both in a way that can create a context for dynamic personal development—and dynamic personal development is required to lead innovative transformative change.

> **Innovating leadership means leaders influence by *equally* engaging their personal intention and action with the organization's culture and systems.**

Though we are, in a sense, defining innovative leadership very broadly, we are also making a distinct point. We are saying that the core aspects that comprise your experience—whether intention, action, cultural, or systematic—are inextricably interconnected. If you affect one aspect, you affect them all.

Innovative leadership is based on the recognition that those four dimensions exist simultaneously in all experiences and already influence every interactive experience we have. So if, for example, you implement a strategy to realign an organization's value system over the next five years, you will also affect personal motivations (intentions), behavioral outcomes, and organizational culture. Influencing one aspect—in this case, functional systems—affects the other aspects, since all four dimensions mutually shape that given occasion. To deny the mutual interplay of any one of the four dimensions misses the full picture. You can only innovate leadership by addressing reality in a comprehensive fashion.

Leadership innovation happens naturally and can be accelerated through the use of a structured process involving your own self-exploration, allowing you to authentically enhance your leadership beyond tactical execution.

To summarize, leadership innovation is the process of improving leadership that allows already successful leaders to raise the bar on their performance and the performance of their organizations.

An innovative leader is defined as someone who consistently delivers results using:

- **Strategic leadership** that inspires individual intentions and *goals* and organizational *vision and culture*;
- **Tactical leadership** that influences an individual's *actions* and the organization's *systems and processes*; and,
- **Holistic leadership** that aligns all core dimensions: *individual intention and action, along with organizational culture and systems.*

The Opportunity of Innovative Leadership

The overwhelming focus of today's organizational changes is on system functionality. Though necessary, it is only part of your total picture. Being guided by more strategically inclusive decisions may be the difference between managing failure and creating tangible success. Your leadership must consider a more balanced definition of innovation that comprehensively aligns vision, teams and systems, and integrates enhanced leadership perspective with system efficiency.

This balanced approach to leadership and innovation is transformative for both you and your organization, and can help you to respond more effectively to challenges within and outside the enterprise. Innovating your leadership gives you the means to successfully adapt in ways that allow optimal performance, even within an organizational climate fraught with continual change and complexity. Conceptually, it synthesizes models from developmental, communications, and systems theory, delivering better insight than singular approaches. Innovative leadership gives you the capacity to openly recognize and critically examine aspects of yourself, as well as your organization's culture and systems, in the midst of any circumstance.

Defining What an Innovative Leader Does

What are specific behaviors that differentiate an innovative leader from a traditional leader? In this time of rapid business, social, and ecological change, a successful innovative leader is one who can continually:

- Clarify and effectively articulate vision
- Link that vision to attainable strategic initiatives
- Develop himself and influence the development of other leaders
- Build effective teams by helping colleagues engage their own leadership strengths
- Cultivate alliances and partnerships
- Anticipate and aggressively respond to both challenges and opportunities
- Develop robust and resilient solutions
- Develop and test hypotheses like a scientist
- Measure, learn, and refine on an ongoing basis

To further illustrate some of the qualities of innovative leadership, we offer this comparison between traditional leadership and innovative leadership:

TRADITIONAL LEADERSHIP	INNOVATIVE LEADERSHIP
Leader is guided primarily by desire for personal success and peripherally by organizational success	Leader is humbly guided by a more altruistic vision of success based on both performance and the value of the organization's positive impact
Leadership decision style is "command and control;" leader has all the answers	Leader leverages team for answers as part of the decision-making process
Leader picks a direction in "black/white" manner; tends to dogmatically stay the course	Leader perceives and behaves like a scientist: continually experimenting, measuring, and testing for improvement and exploring new models and approaches
Leader focuses on being technically correct and in charge	Leader is continually learning and developing self and others
Leader manages people to perform by being autocratic and controlling	Leader motivates people to perform through strategic focus, mentoring and coaching, and interpersonal intelligence
Leader tends to the numbers and primarily utilizes quantitative measures that drive those numbers	Leader tends to financial performance, customer satisfaction, employee engagement, community impact, and cultural cohesion

Getting the Most from the Workbook

Before you get started, take a moment to think about why you purchased this workbook. Setting goals and understanding your intentions and expectations about the exercises will help you focus on identifying and driving your desired results.

In order to help clarify, consider the following questions:

- What are the five to seven events and choices that brought you to where you are professionally and personally?
- How did these events and choices contribute to choosing to buy and use this workbook?
- What stands out in the list you have made? Are there any surprises or patterns?
- What do you hope to gain from your investment in leadership development?
- What meaningful impact will it produce in your professional career and personal life?

In addition to your reflection on the above questions, here are some ideas we recommend to help you get the most out of this experience. It is our experience that people who adhere to the following agreements tend to have a deeper and more enriching overall experience. By participating in this fashion, you will generate a richer evaluation of yourself and most effectively take advantage of what this workbook has to offer.

Take a moment to reflect on the guidelines:

AGREEMENT	RELATED ACTION OR BEHAVIOR
1. Be fully present	Let go of thoughts about other activities while you read. Bring your full attention to the work
2. Take responsibility for your own success	Be 100% responsible for the outcome of your engagement with this material
3. Participate as fully as possible	Complete all the exercises to the best of your abilities. Apply the concepts and skills that work best for you, and modify those that do not
4. Practice good life management	Invest time at scheduled intervals to work on the materials when you are mentally and emotionally at your best
5. Lean into optimal discomfort; take risks without overwhelming yourself	Be candid, open, and direct. Allow yourself to be curious and vulnerable
6. Take the process seriously, and more importantly take yourself lightly. Make this a positive and rewarding experience	Allow yourself balance. Find the lesson and humor in both your successes and mistakes. Most importantly, have fun!

How to Use the Workbook

After this introduction to innovative leadership, each subsequent chapter builds on a series of exercises and reflection questions designed to guide you through the process of developing your own abilities as an innovative leader. We recommend that you use the following sequence to help efficiently process the material:

1. Read Intently

Read through the chapter completely, as we introduce and illustrate an integrated set of concepts for each element in building innovative leadership.

2. Contemplate

Using a set of carefully chosen applications and specifically designed exercises will help you to embody the work and bring the concepts to life. Through a process of dynamic examination and reflection, you will be encouraged to contemplate some significant, real-life implications of change. Many of the exercises can be done on your own; others are designed to be conducted with input from your colleagues.

3. Link Together Your Experience

As you sequentially build your understanding, you will begin noticing habits and conditioned patterns that present you with clear opportunities for growth. Though you may encounter personal resistance along the way, you will also discover new and exciting strengths. As you become more adept at using these ideas, you will find yourself increasingly capable of proactive engagement with the concepts, along with an ability to respond to situations requiring innovative leadership with greater capacity.

Once you have completed the process, you will have created a plan to grow as an innovative leader. Ultimately, implementing that plan will be up to you and your team.

Innovative Leadership Assessment

Following is a short self assessment to help you identify your own innovative leadership scores. It is organized by the five domains of innovative leadership and will give you a general sense of where to focus your efforts to improve your innovative leadership capacity. As you progress through the book, you will find information on the full assessments if you are interested in a more in-depth and thorough analysis of your current capacity.

We encourage you to take this assessment as a way to get a snapshot of where you excel and where you may want to focus your developmental activities and energies.

Score Yourself on Awareness of Leader Type and Self-Management

Think about your level of response to work situations during the past three months:

Never (1)   Rarely (2)   Sometimes (3)   Often (4)   Almost always (5)

1. I have taken a leadership type assessment such as the Enneagram, Myers-Briggs Type Indicator or DISC, and used this information about myself to increase my effectiveness.   **1 2 3 4 5**

2. I use the insight from this assessment to understand my type—specifically, I understand my gifts and limitations, and try to leverage my strengths and manage my limitations.   **1 2 3 4 5**

3. I have a reflection practice where I understand, actively monitor and work with my "fixations" (a fixation is a negative thought pattern).   **1 2 3 4 5**

4. I have a clear sense of who I am and what I want to contribute in the world.   **1 2 3 4 5**

5. I manage my emotional reactions to allow me to respond with socially appropriate behavior.   **1 2 3 4 5**

6. I am aware of what causes me stress and actively manage it.   **1 2 3 4 5**

7. I have positive coping strategies.   **1 2 3 4 5**

8. I actively seek ways to feel empowered even when the organization may not.   **1 2 3 4 5**

Total Score

- If your overall score in this category is 24 or less, it's time to pay attention to your leadership type and self management.

- If your overall score in this category is 25–31, you are in the healthy range, but could still benefit from some focus on your leadership type and self-management.

- If your overall score is 32 or above, Congratulations! You are self-aware and using your leadership type to increase your effectiveness.

Score Yourself on Developmental Perspective Aligned with Innovation

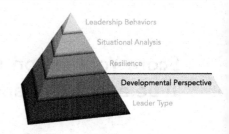

Think about your level of response to work situations during the past three months:
Never (1)   Rarely (2)   Sometimes (3)   Often (4)   Almost always (5)

1. I have a sense of life purpose and do work that is generally aligned with that purpose.   **1 2 3 4 5**

2. I am motivated by the impact I make on the world more than on personal notoriety.   **1 2 3 4 5**

3. I try to live my life according to my personal values.   **1 2 3 4 5**

4. I believe that collaboration across groups and organizations is important to accomplish our goals.   **1 2 3 4 5**

5. I believe that getting business results must be balanced with treating people fairly and kindly as well as have an impact on our customers and community.   **1 2 3 4 5**

6. I seek input from others consistently to test my thinking and expand my perspective.   **1 2 3 4 5**

7. I think about the impact of my work on the many elements of our community and beyond.   **1 2 3 4 5**

8. I am open and curious, always trying new things and learning from all of them.   **1 2 3 4 5**

9. I appreciate the value of rules and am willing to question them in a professional manner in service of meeting our goals and improving the service we provide to our customers.   **1 2 3 4 5**

Total Score

- If your overall score in this category is 27 or less, it's time to pay attention to your developmental level including testing your current level and focusing on developing in the area of developmental perspectives.

- If your overall score in this category is 28–35, you are in the healthy range, but could still benefit from some focus on developing in the area of developmental perspectives.

- If your score is 36 or above, Congratulations! Your developmental level appears to be aligned with innovative leadership, yet this assessment is only a subset of a full assessment.

Score Yourself on Resilience

Think about your level of response to work situations during the past three months:

Never (1)   *Rarely (2)*   *Sometimes (3)*   *Often (4)*   *Almost always (5)*

1. I consistently take care of my physical needs such as getting enough sleep and exercise.   **1 2 3 4 5**

2. I have a sense of purpose and get to do activities that contribute to that purpose daily.   **1 2 3 4 5**

3. I have a high degree of self-awareness and manage my thoughts actively.   **1 2 3 4 5**

4. I have a strong support system consisting of a healthy mix of friends, colleagues, and family.   **1 2 3 4 5**

5. I can reframe challenges to find something of value in most situations.   **1 2 3 4 5**

6. I build strong trusting relationships at work.   **1 2 3 4 5**

7. I am aware of my own self-talk and actively manage it.   **1 2 3 4 5**

8. I have a professional development plan that includes gaining skills and acquiring additional perspectives.   **1 2 3 4 5**

Total Score

- If your overall score in this category is 24 or less, it's time to pay attention to your resilience.

- If your overall score in this category is 25–31, you are in the healthy range, but could still benefit from some focus on resilience.

- If your score is 32 or above, Congratulations! You are likely performing well in the area of resilience, yet this assessment is only a subset of the full resilience assessment.

Score Yourself on Managing Alignment of Self and Organization

Think about your level of response to work situations during the past three months:

Never (1)   Rarely (2)   Sometimes (3)   Often (4)   Almost always (5)

1. I am aware of my own passions and values.   **1 2 3 4 5**

2. My behavior consistently reflects my goals and values.   **1 2 3 4 5**

3. I feel safe pushing back when I am asked to do things that are not aligned   **1 2 3 4 5**
    with my values.

4. I am aware that my behavior and decisions as a leader have a significant   **1 2 3 4 5**
    impact on the organization's structure and culture.

5. I am deliberate about aligning the organization's pay and performance   **1 2 3 4 5**
    systems with the types of behaviors we want to encourage (both results
    and behaviors).

6. The organization's key measures and systems encourage the right actions   **1 2 3 4 5**
    aligned with the culture, and discourage actions that will damage the
    organization or make me uncomfortable.

7. I am aware of how my values align with those of the organization and where   **1 2 3 4 5**
    we are misaligned; I take steps to encourage changes in the culture such as
    talking about our values and reinforcing what we say we care about.

Total Score

◢ If your overall score in this category is 21 or less, it's time to pay attention to your alignment with the organization and also the alignment of culture and systems within the organization that you are able to impact.

◢ If your overall score in this category is 22–27, you are in the healthy range, but could still benefit from some focus on alignment.

◢ If your score is 28 or above, Congratulations! You are well-aligned with the organization and the organization's culture and systems are well-aligned.

Score Yourself on Leadership Behaviors

Think about your level of response to work situations during the past three months:

Never (1)   *Rarely (2)*   *Sometimes (3)*   *Often (4)*   *Almost always (5)*

1. I tend to be proactive—I anticipate what is coming next and actively manage it. Depending on role, this may happen primarily in my personal life.   **1 2 3 4 5**

2. I focus on creating results in a way that encourages others to grow and develop while accomplishing their tasks.   **1 2 3 4 5**

3. I think about the impact of my actions on the overall organization rather than just getting the job done.   **1 2 3 4 5**

4. I see how my work contributes to the overall organizational success and deliberately try to improve myself and the organization.   **1 2 3 4 5**

5. I take time to mentor others—even when I am busy.   **1 2 3 4 5**

6. I consider myself a personal learner because of the time I spend reading and trying new ideas and activities. I am curious.   **1 2 3 4 5**

7. I have the courage to speak out in a professional manner when asked to do something I disagree with.   **1 2 3 4 5**

8. I accomplish results by working with and through others in a positive and constructive manner.   **1 2 3 4 5**

Total Score

- If your overall score in this category is 24 or less, it's time to pay attention to your leadership behaviors and look for ways to develop in alignment with your goals.

- If your overall score in this category is 25–31, you are in the healthy range, but could still benefit from some focus on your leadership behaviors.

- If your score is 32 or above, Congratulations! You are likely performing well in the area of leadership behaviors, but this assessment is only a subset of a full leadership behavior assessment.

CHAPTER 1
Elements of Innovative Leadership

We will start with a discussion of innovative leadership then go into what nonprofit leaders do in chapter two. This chapter provides the general framework for innovating how you lead. Innovative leadership is comprised of the five elements presented and discussed below then these are applied throughout the balance of the book.

Figure 1-1 Five Elements of Innovative Leadership

- Leadership Behaviors
- Situational Analysis
- Resilience
- Developmental Perspective
- Leader Type

The five elements of innovative leadership are reflected in Figure1-1.

What is truly unique in this approach to leadership is the overall comprehensiveness of the model. Theorists have looked at each of these elements separately over many years, and have suggested that mastering one or two of them is typically sufficient for effective leaders. We believe that while that may have been true in a less complex world, it is no longer the case. As the twenty-first century unfolds, the most effective leaders will need a much more holistic view than at any other time in history. In the following chapter, we will define and describe each individual element of innovative leadership and how they interact.

Leader Type

Part of the challenge in innovating leadership is learning to become more introspective and put that introspective knowledge into practice. Looking inside yourself, examining the make-up of your inner being, enables you to function in a highly grounded way, rather than operating from the innate biases that lead to uninformed or unconscious decision-making.

First and foremost, when thinking about leadership, start by simply considering your disposition, tendencies, inclinations, and ways of thinking and acting. Innovating leadership hinges on understanding the simple manner in which you live in your life. One way to observe this is by examining aspects of your inner being, often called leader type, which reflect the leader's personality type. The Leader Personality Type (referred to going forward as Leader Type) has a critical influence on who you are as a leader. It is an essential foundation of your personal make-up and greatly shapes your leadership effectiveness. The ancient adage of "know thyself," attributed to various Greek philosophers, holds true as a crucial underpinning in leadership performance.

Your ability to use deep introspection relies on your development of a capacity for self-understanding and self-awareness. Both allow you to expand your perspective as well as build a greater understanding of others. These critical traits associated with leader type support a leader's abilities to manage self, communicate effectively with others, and encourage personal learning. You can use your understanding of your leader type (understanding yourself and others) as a powerful tool in effective leadership.

It is important to keep in mind that this particular notion of type is something that is native to your being and generally does not change significantly over the course of your life. This is an essential point: by understanding your type, as well as that of others around you, you can begin to see situations without the bias of your own perceptions. You have a clearer understanding, and can thus make more informed decisions with less speculation. You learn to deeply understand the inner movements of your strengths, weaknesses, and core patterns. Leadership typing tools are helpful in promoting this kind of self-knowledge and pattern recognition.

> *By learning about these patterns, you can gain perspective on your life and start connecting the dots among your different experiences. Most of us have a concept about how we behave, but that idea is likely clouded and not entirely true. One of the hardest things for most people is to see themselves accurately. How astonishing it is to see through the clouds and recognize yourself clearly.*
>
> — Roxanne Howe-Murphy, *Deep Living*

Learning at this deeper level from your own inner dynamics can offer remarkable insight into areas of your life that, in your own personal experience, you may either exaggerate or under emphasize.

Self-awareness and the capacity for self-management are foundational to innovative leadership and overall leadership effectiveness. By becoming aware of your inherent gifts as well as those of others, you are able to improve your personal effectiveness and that of the teams and departments with which you work.

Developmental Perspective

In this workbook we will be talking about *developmental levels and perspectives* as a core element in developing innovative leadership. Developmental perspectives significantly influence how you see your role and function in the workplace, how you interact with other people, and how you solve problems. The term *developmental perspective* can be described as "meaning making" or how you make meaning or sense of experiences. This is important because the algorithm you use to make sense of the world influences your thoughts and actions. Incorporating these perspectives as part of your inner exploration is critical to developing innovative leadership. In his best-selling business book *Good to Great*, author Jim Collins refers to Level 5 Leadership as an example of developmental perspectives applied to leadership. While we do not cover the relationship of Level 5 Leadership to developmental perspectives in this workbook, you can find more information on this subject in the Innovative Leadership Fieldbook.

Figure 1-2 Enneagram & Developmental Perspectives

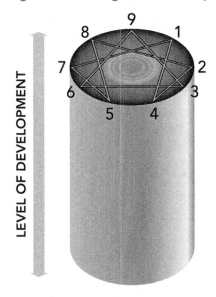

In order to connect developmental perspective with leader type, let's look at how these models come together. While leader type is generally constant over your life, you have the capacity to grow and develop your leadership perspective. In fact, leadership research strongly suggests that although your inherent leader type determines your tendency to lead, good leaders also develop over time. Therefore, it is often the case that leaders are perhaps both born and made. How leaders are made is best described using an approach that considers developmental perspective. Type remains consistent during your life while developmental perspective evolves. This is an important differentiator in leadership effectiveness and allows you to see what can be changed and what should be accepted as innate personality type.

We can also apply this model to the organizational level to help select and train leaders more effectively. Here are some additional benefits of using a model of developmental perspective:

- It guides leaders in determining their personal development goals and action plans using developmental perspectives as an important criteria.

- It is important to consider when determining which individuals and team members best fit specific roles.

- It helps in identifying high-potential leaders to groom for growth opportunities.

- It helps in the hiring process to determine individual fit for a specific job.

- It helps change agents understand the perspective of others and craft solutions that meet the needs of all stakeholders.

Figure 1-3 Maslow's Hierarchy of Needs

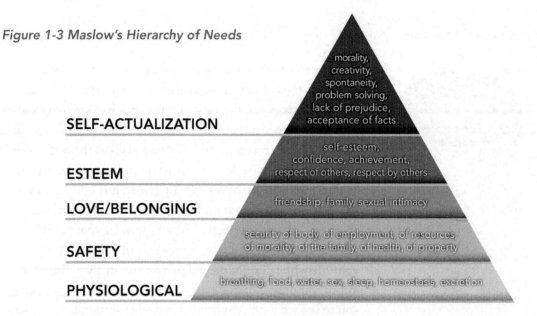

The developmental perspective approach is based on research and observation that, over time, people tend to grow and progress through a number of very distinct stages of awareness and ability. One of the most well-known and tested developmental models is Abraham Maslow's Hierarchy of Needs, a pyramid-shaped visual aid Maslow created to help explain his theory of psychological and physical human needs. As you ascend the steps of the pyramid you can eventually reach a level of self-actualization.

Developmental growth occurs much like other capabilities grow in your life. Building on your leader type, you continue to grow, increasing access to or capacity for additional skills. We call this "transcend and include" in that you transcend the prior level/perspective and still maintain the ability to function at that perspective. Let us use the example of learning how to run to illustrate the process of development. You must first learn to stand and walk before you can run. And yet, as you eventually master running, you still effortlessly retain the earlier, foundational skill that allowed you to stand and walk. In other words, you can develop your capacity to build beyond the basic skills you have now by moving through more progressive stages. It is also important to note that while individuals develop the ability to run, there are many times that walking is a much more appropriate choice of movement. The successful leader has a broad repertoire of behavior and is able to select the most appropriate one depending on the situation.

People develop through stages at vastly differing rates, often influenced by significant events or "disorienting dilemmas." Those events or dilemmas provide opportunities to begin experiencing your world from a completely different point-of-view. The nature of those influential events can vary greatly, ranging from positive social occasions like marriage, a new job or the birth of a child to negative experiences, such as job loss, an accident or death of a loved one. These situations may often trigger more lasting changes in your way of thinking and feeling altogether. New developmental perspectives can develop very gradually over time or, in some cases, emerge quite abruptly.

Some developmentally advanced people may be relatively young and yet others may experience very little developmental growth over the course of their life. Adding to the complexity of developmental growth is the fact that the unfolding of developmental perspectives is not predictably based on age, gender, nationality or affluence. We can sense indicators that help us identify developmental perspective when we listen and exchange ideas with others, employ introspection, and display openness to learning. In fact, most people very naturally intuit and discern what motivates others as well as what causes some of their greatest challenges.

We believe a solid understanding of developmental perspectives is critical to innovating leadership and encourage you to delve into this concept in much greater detail. The purpose of this workbook is to introduce you to the concepts.

Resilience

There are two distinct ways to understand resilience. First, using an engineering analogy, resilience is viewed as how much disturbance your systems can absorb before a breakdown. This view highlights the sturdiness of individual systems. Second, from a leadership perspective, resilience can be viewed as the ability to adapt in the face of erratic change while continuing to be both fluid in approach and driven towards attaining strategic goals. The first definition reflects stability and the second refers to fluidity and endurance. Addressing all aspects of resilience is critical to optimizing it.

Among the elements essential to leadership, resilience is unique in that it integrates the physical and psychological aspects of leader type and developmental perspective to create the foundation of a leader's inner stability. This foundation enables you to demonstrate fluidity and endurance as you adapt to ongoing change.

Figure 1-4 Elements of Resilience

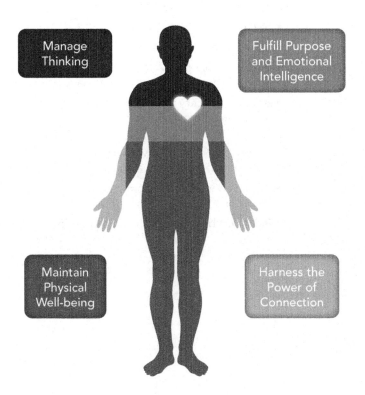

The underlying premise of resilience is: as a leader, you need to be physically and emotionally healthy to do a good job. In addition to physical and emotional health, the resilient leader also has a clear sense of life purpose, strong emotional intelligence, and strong supportive relationships. For most people, enhancing resilience requires a personal change.

Our model has four categories, shown in Figure 1-4. They are: maintain physical well-being, manage thinking, fulfill purpose using emotional intelligence, and harness the power of connection. These categories are interlinked, and all of them must be in balance to create long-term resilience.

Leaders we work with often initially say they are too busy to take care of themselves. Finding the balance between self-care and meeting all of our daily commitments is tough. Most people fall short of their goals and over the longer term make choices for or against their resilience and personal health. Our message here is that creating and maintaining resilience is essential to your success. As you improve your resilience, you will think more clearly and have a greater positive impact in your interactions with others; investing in your resilience supports the entire organization's effectiveness.

The following table provides questions for each of the four resilience categories to identify opportunities for improvement.

TABLE 1-1 KEYS TO BUILDING & RETAINING PERSONAL RESILIENCE

Maintain Physical Well-being	**Fulfill Life Purpose**
Are you getting enough: - Sleep - Exercise - Healthy Food - Time in nature - Time to meditate & relax Are you limiting or eliminating: - Caffeine - Nicotine	Understand what you stand for. Maintain focus. Ask: - What is my purpose? - Why is it important to me? - What values do I hold that will enable me to accomplish my purpose? - What opportunities do I have in my professional life that help me achieve my life purpose?
Manage Thoughts	**Harness the Power of Connection**
Practice telling yourself: - Challenges are normal and healthy for any individual or organization - My current problem is a doorway to an innovative solution - I feel inspired about the opportunity to create new possibilities that did not exist before	Practice effective communication: - Say things simply, and clearly - Make communication safe by being responsive - Encourage people to ask questions and clarify if they do not understand your message - Balance advocacy for your point with inquiring about the other persons' points - When you have a different point of view, seek to understand how and why the other person believes what they do in a non-threatening way - When in doubt, share information and emotions - Build trust by acting for the greater good

Situational Analysis

Though much of the work of building innovative leadership is based on an in-depth examination of your personal and professional experience, understanding the background or context of that experience is equally important. Consider that your experience isn't merely a collection of personal expressions, events, and random happenstance; rather, it is fundamentally shaped by the background interplay of your individual attributes, shared relationships, and involved organizations.

Every moment of experience is influenced by a mutual interaction of self, culture, action, and systems. All four of these basic dimensions are fundamental to every experience we have. Situational analysis involves evaluating the four-dimensional view of reality shown in Figure 1-5. This comprehensive approach ensures all dimensions are aligned resulting in balanced and efficient action. We refer to these four dimensions as self, action, culture, and systems. This balancing without favoring elements is an important skill for innovative leaders.

Leaders often take a partial approach to changing organizations. They over-emphasize systems change with little or no consideration to the culture or how their personal views and actions shape the content and success of the change. This multi-dimensional approach provides a more complete and accurate view of events and situations. Situational analysis enables you to create alignment across the four dimensions on an ongoing basis.

Figure 1-5- Integral Model

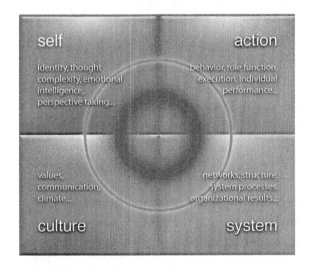

American-born philosopher Ken Wilber developed a conceptual scheme to illustrate the four basic dimensions of being that form the backbone of experience. His Integral Model provides a map that shows the mutual relationship and interconnection among four dimensions where each represents basic elements of human experience.

When you use situational analysis, you are cultivating simultaneous awareness of all four dimensions. Let's look at an example. This is a sample narrative taken from Integral Life Practice (Wilber et al) that will give you a more experiential description of how these dimensions shape every situation in your life.

Example: *"Visualize yourself walking into an office building in the morning..."*

Self *(Upper-Left Quadrant, "I"):* You feel excited and a little nervous about the big meeting today. Thoughts race through your head about how best to prepare.

Culture *(Lower-Left Quadrant, "We"):* You enter a familiar office culture of shared meaning, values, and expectations that are communicated, explicitly and implicitly, every day.

Action *(Upper-Right, "It")*: Your physical behaviors are obvious: walking, waving good morning, opening a door, sitting down at your desk, turning on the computer, and so on. Brain activity, heart rate, and perspiration all increase as the important meeting draws nearer.

System *(Lower-Right, "Its")*: Elevators, powered by electricity generated miles away, lift you to your floor. You easily navigate the familiar office environment, arrive at your desk, and log on to the organization's intranet to check the latest sales numbers within the organization's several international markets.

In applying situational analysis to an organizational change, you would be aware of the four dimensions as referenced above and, when changing one, you would consider the impact on the others. If you get promoted and want to be perceived differently, how will you behave in the situation above? What will be different in all four dimensions as you walk into the office building?

A crucial part of innovating leadership is developing your capacity to be aware of all dimensions of reality in any given moment and identify misalignments. Even though you cannot physically see the values, beliefs, and emotions that strongly influence the way an individual colleague perceives himself/herself and the world, nor a group's culture, emotional climate or collective perception, they still profoundly shape the vision and potential of leaders to innovate.

Situational Analysis is an innovative leadership tool that allows you not only to make more informed decisions, but also helps you optimize performance within yourself, your teams, and the broader organization. The alignment of all dimensions is the key to optimizing performance.

Leader Behaviors

Let's now shift our focus to the actionable craft of leadership as observable skills and behaviors. In this section, we are talking about observable leadership skills and behaviors and hard skills and their associated behaviors. Leadership skills and hard skills are critical to success, and serve as objective performance measures of innovative leadership.

Hard skills fall into two primary categories: industry-related knowledge, skills, and aptitudes; and functional knowledge, skills, and aptitudes. Leadership skills can be evaluated by observable behaviors and result from knowledge, skills, and aptitudes specifically related to the craft of leadership.

We will be using the term leadership behaviors in this workbook when referring to leadership knowledge, skills, and aptitudes and the resulting behaviors. Both hard skills and leadership behaviors are critical to building innovative leadership; however, the balance between the importance of hard skills and leadership behaviors will shift as the leader progresses in the organization with leadership skills and behaviors becoming increasingly important with career advancement.

Leadership behaviors are important because they are the objective actions the leader takes that impact organizational success. We have all seen brilliant leaders behave in a manner that damages their organization and we have seen other leaders continually behave in ways that promote ongoing organizational success. Effective leadership behaviors drive organizational success and, conversely, ineffective leadership behaviors drive organizational dysfunction or failure. Even the most functionally brilliant leader must demonstrate effective leadership behaviors to be successful when leading an organization.

An example of the need for both hard skills and leadership behaviors is a hospital CEO client. To be successful, this CEO must possess the hard skills in nonprofit administration to understand how the organization operates and the leadership behaviors to be able to effectively lead. If either of these sets of skills is missing, the leader and the nonprofit are at risk of failure. Early in his career, a mastery of nonprofit administration set him apart from his peers. As he progressed into the senior leadership ranks and ultimately to the role of CEO, his use of leadership behaviors became his primary focus while he never lost the need for hard skills, now he relies on his functional and leadership skills to guide his direction and action.

There are different ways to discuss leadership from a skills perspective as demonstrated by Peter Northouse in his book on leadership.

> *There are several strengths in conceptualizing leadership from a skills [actions] perspective. First, it is a leader-centered model that stresses the importance of the leader's abilities, and it places learning skills at the center of effective leadership performance. Second, the skills approach describes leadership in such a way that it makes it available to everyone. Skills are behaviors that we all can learn to develop and improve. Third, the skills approach provides a sophisticated map that explains how effective leadership performance can be achieved.*
>
> *— Peter G. Northouse, Leadership Theory and Practice*

As a leader, it is important to understand the key leadership behaviors important to you and your organization. With this understanding, you can determine where you excel and where you may want to refine your skills.

The Leadership Circle Profile (LCP) Behaviors

Figure 1-6- The Leadership Circle Profile

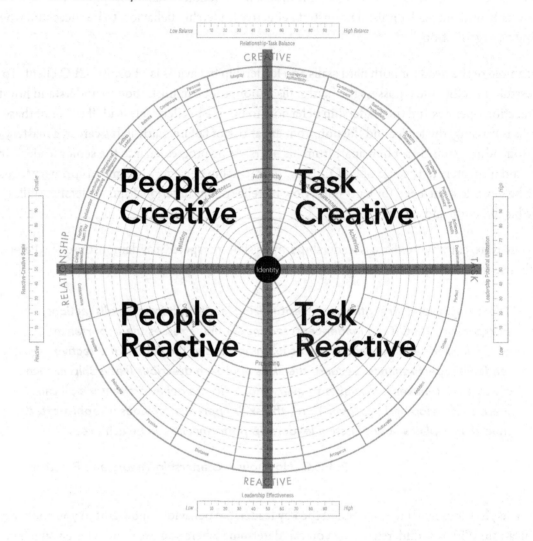

The Leadership Circle measures key dimensions of leadership shown in the inner circle in Figure 1-6. The sub-categories are shown in the outer circle (for reference go to www.theleadershipcircle.com) and can be broken into four key dimensions: people creative, task creative, people reactive, and task reactive. These four categories are created by drawing a line through the circle horizontally to separate the creative and reactive dimensions. The second line is drawn vertically to separate the people and task dimensions. The top of the circle behaviors are *creative behaviors*:

- ◢ Relating
- ◢ Self-awareness
- ◢ Authenticity
- ◢ Systems Awareness
- ◢ Achieving

These behaviors reflect proactive action which is referred to by the Leadership Circle as "Creative." These behaviors reflect behaviors associated with setting strategic direction and inspiring people to accomplish goals.

The behaviors in the bottom half of the circle are ***reactive behaviors***. They reflect <u>inner beliefs that limit effectiveness, authentic expression, and empowering leadership</u>. These dimensions reflect behaviors associated with following direction or reacting to circumstances as they arise rather than setting direction and creating the conditions for success.

The creative and reactive dimensions are then split on the vertical axis between people and task behaviors. People behaviors are associated with the actions leaders take to build themselves and their people such as relating and self-awareness. The task behaviors are actions leaders take associated with the work of running a business, such as systems awareness and achieving. The degree of emphasis on task versus relating will vary depending on your level within the organization, the overall organizational structure, and the organizational type. What is important to note is that leadership requires a balance of task-related behaviors along with relationship-related behaviors and this balance changes depending on the situation.

It is important to understand the behaviors associated with innovative leadership and also be able to flex your own leadership behaviors to match what is required by the organization. The most effective leaders and organizations demonstrate behaviors heavily weighted on the creative end of the scale. The balance between task and relationship will depend in part on the role of the leader within the organization. Strong leaders have the capacity to perform both people and task-related roles well.

According to *The Leadership Circle Participant Profile Manual,* 2009 Edition published by The Leadership Circle, "These competencies [behaviors] have been well researched and shown to be the most critical behaviors and skill sets for leaders." Table 1-2 was adapted from *The Leadership Circle Participant Profile Manual,* 2009 Edition, published by The Leadership Circle.

TABLE 1-2 LCP DIMENSION DEFINITIONS

Creative leadership behaviors listed below reflect key behaviors and internal assumptions that lead to <u>high fulfillment, high achievement leadership</u>.

The **Relating** Dimension measures leader capability to relate to others in a way that brings out the best in people, groups and organizations. It is composed of:

- Caring Connection
- Fosters Team Play
- Collaborator
- Mentoring and Developing
- Interpersonal Intelligence

The **Self-Awareness** Dimension measures the leader's orientation to ongoing professional and personal development, as well as the degree to which inner self-awareness is expressed through high integrity leadership. It is composed of:

- Selfless Leader
- Balance
- Composure
- Personal Learner

TABLE 5-1 LCP DIMENSION DEFINITIONS (CONT.)

The **Authenticity** Dimension measures the leader's capability to relate to others in an authentic, courageous, and high integrity manner. It is composed of: ▪ Integrity ▪ Authenticity	The **Systems Awareness** Dimension measures the degree to which the leader's awareness is focused on whole system improvement and on community welfare (the symbiotic relationship between the long-term welfare of the community and the interests of the organization). It is composed of: ▪ Community Concern ▪ Sustainable Productivity ▪ Systems Thinker
The **Achieving** Dimension measures the extent to which the leader offers visionary, authentic, and high accomplishment leadership. It is composed of: ▪ Strategic Focus ▪ Purposeful and Visionary ▪ Achieves Results ▪ Decisiveness	

We will use these creative behaviors throughout the book as we refer to leadership behavior.

Since this book is about becoming an innovative nonprofit leader, chapter two focuses on defining the role of an effective nonprofit CEO in a community based-organization. Performing this role well is the foundation upon which to build innovative leadership. If you find developmental opportunities in this chapter, please make sure you add them to your development plan along with the other areas of innovative leadership development. Additionally, there is an appendix that provides additional details on nonprofit leadership and management for the leader who wants to explore a specific topic in more detail.

Developing Innovative Leadership

Chapters three through seven walk you through the process of developing innovative leadership specifically for nonprofits. Each chapter reflects one step in the development process and includes tools, templates, questions for reflection, and an example of a person who has completed the process. It is the comprehensiveness of this reflection coupled with the exercises that will give you insight into yourself and your organization. This insight is required to change yourself and your organization concurrently or to manage your internal change in the context of an organization that you cannot or do not want to change. It is important to note that leadership development is an ongoing process. Upon completion of this process you will be more effective; yet, depending on your objectives, you may still want to continue developing. Figure 1-7 below shows the six steps.

Figure 1-7 Leadership Development Process

While this process appears linear, we have found that when leaders work through these steps they often return to earlier parts of the process to clarify and sometimes change details they had originally thought were correct. The structure of our process will continue to challenge you to refine the work you have accomplished in prior tasks. First ideas are often good ones, but when you work with this tool you will continually find insight and discover new things. We encourage you to continue to test your ideas and feel comfortable going back in the process for further refinement.

The time you spend working on the workbook is an investment in your development. If you are engaging deeply in the process it will likely take you three to six months or longer to complete. Whether managing either personal and organizational change, or internal change alone in the context of an organization that you cannot or do not want to change, reflection and thorough evaluation are required. This reflection will take time and is critical to your growth. We strongly encourage you to engage in the process with as much time and attention as possible. The value you ultimately take from this process is closely linked to the time you invest.

REFLECTION QUESTIONS

What innovative challenges does your organization face?

How does your organization support effective leadership for innovation?

In what ways would you consider yourself an innovative leader?

How do you personally connect with leadership and innovation?

Where are the opportunities for you to be an innovative leader?

What would make you and your organization more effective in leading innovation beyond products, services, and systems?

CHAPTER 2
Fulfilling the Role of a Nonprofit Leader

To ensure we are starting from a common foundation, we will first explore the essentials of nonprofit leadership, including the role of the CEO (alternately called executive director or president and CEO) and how that role impacts the development of the board of directors. We will then discuss how to innovate nonprofit leadership. Our intent is to demonstrate how the innovative leadership model can be used to transform your leadership and, by extension, the nonprofit you lead. One of the foundational beliefs of innovating leadership is that the leader is already effectively leading an organization. Building innovative leadership involves influencing others by engaging your intentions and actions, along with the organization's culture and systems.

There are several elements of the innovative leadership model that are not directly addressed in this chapter, such as building self-awareness and resilience. While these are not discussed directly, they are embedded in behaviors and are critical for the nonprofit leader to sustain productivity and long-term results. For example, developing resilience will better allow the CEO to meet the daily challenges of the role.

A core element of innovative leadership is aligning your values to your leadership behaviors, and to your life. Nonprofit organizations are typically centered around values. The shared value among nonprofit organizations is of making the world a better place, of engagement, and of service to humanity in whatever form that service takes. The values of its leaders impact the culture and the values of all organizations.

While the overall book is about nonprofit leadership, we believe it is important to discuss the role of the nonprofit CEO. The CEO engages in a blend of leadership, management, and tasks on a daily basis. The mix of these three elements depends on the size and complexity of the organization, the staff size, the organizational structure, and, in many cases, the amount of funding. As we explore the role of the CEO, you will notice that some of the activities are management or task-oriented, while the remaining exercises are more leadership-based.

Nonprofit leaders must deal with a high degree of complexity as well as be aligned with the organization they lead. Small to medium-size nonprofit CEOs often deal with a much higher degree of complexity than their business counterparts because they interact with governing boards, manage multiple income streams with a variety of intents, and often meet government grant reporting requirements that privately held businesses do not. A 501 (c) 3 nonprofit status is a tax status that does not in any way diminish the professionalism and responsibility of its leaders.

The role of a nonprofit CEO differs across agencies, and this chapter is not intended to be a cookie cutter plan for how to lead an agency. CEO capacities are as different as the expectations that individual CEOs may be expected to meet. Boards of directors are as different as the various roles that board may serve. Even the variety, scope, and type of nonprofit organizations are diverse.

For the purpose of clarity, our focus will be on the role of nonprofit community organizations, as opposed to association or professional organizations, and to governing boards, as opposed to advisory boards. We lay out what we believe are the variety of roles a CEO is likely to find in any given community organization. Your observations will likely be different based on the institutions and differing personalities serving the leadership roles.

The CEO is responsible for leading, managing, coordinating, and/or implementing the items listed below. Although the wording is different, each of these responsibilities is aligned with one or more leadership behaviors on the Leadership Circle Profile with the exception of board development and CEO partnership which encompasses all of the leadership behaviors.

1. Board development and board CEO partnership

2. Strategic thinking and planning

3. Resource development and management

4. Staff leadership and development

5. Program development, implementation, and evaluation

6. Policy, plan, and procedure development

7. Inspiration and engagement

Board Development and Board CEO Partnership

A large component of the CEO's role is board development. CEOs should meet individually with members of their board at least annually, with members of the executive committee quarterly, and with the chair twice a month. CEOs serve as ex officio (non-voting member) on all board committees and attend, when possible, relevant committee meetings. The most effective CEOs spend a significant amount of their time on board-related efforts. For a developing board, a much greater commitment of time will be required.

The role of the board is integral to the role of the CEO. Board members will join the board with a diverse understanding of board governance; as such, the CEO will often be managing up.

Boards of directors are responsible for governance, which includes:

Mission, Vision, and Strategic Planning	- The mission statement answers why the organization exists - A vision statement describes what the organization will look like at a specified time in the future - Strategic planning is a process by which the board, staff, and select constituents decide the strategy for the future direction of an organization and allocate resources, including people, to ensure that target is reached
Serving as the Fiduciary Responsible Agent	- Fiscal understanding and formal approval of finances, audits, and the IRS tax form 990, as well as safeguarding the community's resources and ensuring accountability and transparency - Understanding how a program fills a need in the community, what that programming is, how it is evaluated, and the number of clients that are served
Set Policy	The board sets all polices and approves all plans. Please see the policy, plan, and procedure development section toward the end of this chapter for a full list of board-approved policies and plans
Raise Money	The board sets the tone for a culture of philanthropy by financially supporting the organization, making "the ask" and opening doors for large (as defined by the organization) gifts and sponsorships
Hire, Support, and Evaluate the CEO	The board is responsible for hiring the CEO, setting expectations, and evaluating performance against those expectations

Board Development

Board development is the process by which the board is perpetuated, evaluated, and educated, and is usually implemented through a committee either of the same name or "nominating" or "governance." This committee helps develop an effective board through its two main functions:

Board Building: A diverse board of directors (thought, skill, race, faith, ability, orientation, age, and gender) that is passionate about the mission of the organization is created through a board building process. That process includes an assessment of the current board and needed skill sets, identification of prospective members, recruitment, nomination, and orientation of new board members.

Board Education: Board members will fully understand and can effectively fulfill their commitments to the board of directors when a comprehensive orientation, continuing education, and annual evaluation process is in place.

A board development plan is very helpful to outline the process of prospecting, recruitment, orientation, education, recognition, and evaluation. This plan can also include job descriptions for board members, officers and committee chairs, the chart of work for each committee, and applicable excerpts for the By-laws/Code of Regulations which dictate quorum requirements and length of terms, including whether those terms are renewable. Conflict of Interest policies and forms that each board member completes on an annual basis can also be included and will protect the agency by ensuring that board members do not personally benefit from their service.

CEOs Role in Board Development

The CEO's role in board development is to understand the work of the board and its processes, and support the implementation of each. CEOs play a primary role in building the board. As such, they get the board they build—and have the opportunity to assemble a board that can take the organization to new heights. The CEO assists in building the board that she will ultimately report to. There are very talented people who do not make good board members, as they may not share the agency's core values or may not be a good fit for the team. The CEO makes recommendations, staffs board committees, and supports the board's success, but does not have the authority to add board members. In the case of board development, she should also:

- Support the recruitment of potential board members; arrange and attend meetings with prospective board members and the board or committee chair; share the agency's vision, mission, and board processes, including time, giving and getting expectations, assess the capacity of a prospective member to fit on the team;

- Manage the board development process, including spreadsheet of terms of office;

- Ensure board training and evaluation.

Board Meeting Process

Board members join with a varied understanding of voting procedures and the CEO may have to ensure proper process is followed. It is the CEO, and not usually the board, who is present during a government or independent audit. As such, it is sometimes the CEO who ensures that voting procedures are followed. These procedures are verified during a government or independent audit process, with findings presented to the full board at a future date.

Please see the appendix for suggestions on votes needed, board member criteria, succession planning, appropriate voting procedures, by-laws, and committee structure.

A typical board meeting may include reports from committee chairs and board members having robust discussions about the issues at hand—the premise of those issues and their alignment with the strategic direction of the organization—with the CEO talking (but, not monopolizing the conversation), answering questions, and making recommendations. There is a tendency, especially among new CEOs, to build weaker boards that are more likely to follow all of the CEO's recommendations. This is, obviously, an urge that must be resisted.

Board President and CEO Relationship

When a new board president is appointed, engage her three to six months in advance of assuming that role. When she takes office, she and the CEO should sit down together and map out:

- goals for the term
- the process and define criteria for how the CEO will be evaluated
- a measurement plan defining how success will be gauged and how frequently it is measured
- clear boundaries and responsibilities of each of the roles and a preferred method of contact
- a collaboration plan defining how often to meet to discuss relevant issues, problems, and successes, as well as progress toward goals and/or the strategic plan.

Occasionally, a CEO will run into a board president who believes his job is to run the organization, and that the CEO's job is to function as a department head. In a case such as this, having ethical integrity and a strong relationship with other board members is critical. Most CEOs know that they serve at the pleasure of the board and that significant disagreements may put their employment at risk. Conflicts will likely be prompted by the souring of the board/CEO relationship or a decision made by the board that is in conflict with the CEO's values and ethics, or the law. These challenges are more likely to happen when a CEO and board president do not have a common understanding of their roles.

Most CEOs prefer that board presidents, as well as other board members, do not assign work to the staff directly, but, instead, work through the CEO. The CEO may have to request that, formally. If that is not feasible, staff requests can be made via e-mail and copied to the CEO. Staff initiated board contact should follow the same process. CEOs cannot be held accountable for managing a staff taking directions from others, and the staff will become confused about who to take direction from and whose direction takes priority.

Most board presidents will be the CEO's biggest fan and staunchest defender. In return, the CEO's job is to support a board president in doing her job and protect her from looking stupid. Together, CEOs and board presidents are a powerhouse team that set the path for the agency's success!

Everything cascades from a strong board of directors, including professionally developed, well-regarded, and very successful CEOs, quality programs, and a significant resource development program. CEOs can do a lot on willpower alone—but they can do much more with a powerful board. As previously stated, CEOs will be most successful when they build a strong board and then allow that board to do its job.

Strategic Thinking and Planning

Strategic planning is a process in which the board, staff, and select constituents decide the future direction of an organization and allocate resources, including people, to ensure that target goals are reached. Having a board-approved, staff-involved strategic plan that includes effective measurements and the allocation of resources aligns the organization, provides direction to all levels of staff and board, and defines the path for the future of the organization. It also allows leadership, both board and staff, to reject divergent paths that will not lead to the organization's intended destination.

The CEO's role is to implement the strategic plan, operationalize it for the staff, and manage the board committees toward completing their assignments. It is very easy for CEOs to get pulled into the day to day operations and begin to manage by crisis; however, crisis management is a short term activity and should not become a leadership style. Crisis management, by its definition, doesn't allow for strategic thinking or the opportunity to innovate leadership.

Strategic thinking is an important element of innovating leadership, as innovative leaders inspire the organizational vision and culture that guides individual action. The leader understands what she thinks and believes, which informs and aligns with the organization's culture and that culture aligns with the organization's systems by defining how people within that system behave. These all flow from the strategic plan.

Resource Development and Management

Ultimately, organizations should play a prominent role in serving the community. Resource development is a value proposition that communicates the need an organization addresses. Investors, also known as donors, support the organization after the agency has identified the issues facing its constituents, created solutions to address those issues and measured the impact of those solutions.

Resource development planning allows an organization to lay out its goals for the year and develop a strategy, budget, reporting, evaluation, and monitoring process to create a path to reach those goals. Resource development includes fund-raising, friend-raising, and the solicitation and procurement of in-kind services.

Substantial gifts require substantial dreams—and the capacity to engage people to help reach those dreams. Organizations raise money to support operations, build buildings, create or grow endowments, introduce a new program or expand a current program. It is important to define how much money is needed to reach an organization's goals.

Depending on the goal, there may be one board committee—in the case of an annual campaign—or several board committees—as in the case of a capital campaign. Resource development staff serve on, but do not chair, all fund-raising committees. Committees are responsible for prospecting, cultivating, soliciting, and stewarding lists, and creating a process to move potential donors across those lists.

Plans are developed by the committee to meet the goal. Plans include: committee creation and assignments; donor recognition opportunities; fund-raising goals by area, including grants, individual giving, major donor development, events, etc.; the creation of a case statement, also known as a case for support; assignments and timelines.

Nonprofit fund-raising creates the potential for issues to arise, and the values of the leader and organization will be critical in managing such issues. Most nonprofits seek donors and sponsors. At some point, there will be a conflict between the mission of the nonprofit and the reputation, earned or unfair, of the potential sponsor or donor. Some donors and sponsors will be better for the mission than others. A gift acceptance policy guides the acceptance of gifts and helps to determine what's best for an organization. A clause in the naming rights procedure can also ensure the power to remove a name should a criminal, civil, or public relations issue arise for that donor or company in which the nonprofit finds it necessary to distance itself. For example, several buildings in Houston, Texas, were once named after Ken Lay and Enron. After indictments of corporate abuse and fraud, and the subsequent collapse of Enron, many buildings were renamed.

Money, once raised, needs to be managed appropriately. Any money given for a specific purpose needs to be considered restricted and must be booked and spent accordingly. In other words, if a donor gives you $50 to buy basketballs for the pre-school, you have to buy basketballs for the pre-school. Three basketballs cost $45. You either have to buy another basketball with $10 of unrestricted money, or go back to the donor to ask to use the $5 for something else. For this reason, some organizations have policies that do not allow the acceptance of a restricted gift under a certain dollar amount. This example is an oversimplification, but it highlights the need for good financial systems, honest and ethical policies, and a board, CEO, and directors of finance and development who uphold the organization's values and work together to accept and manage gifts appropriately.

Resource development functions most effectively in a culture of servant leadership and philanthropy among the board and leadership team, as well as an agency-wide commitment. A community cannot and will not invest in an agency without the investment of the board and staff. Development staff cannot raise money without the support of the CEO. CEOs cannot raise money without the support of the board. Resource development is a group effort, with everyone giving, and everyone moving toward the goal of a sustainable organization.

Staff Management, Leadership, and Development

All staff in a nonprofit are ultimately responsible to the CEO and the CEO is ultimately responsible to the board. The CEO sets the tone, holds people accountable, provides direction, supervision, and guidance, motivates and inspires, ensures that policies and procedures are implemented fairly, impacts the culture, and ensures that their own and the agency's values are upheld. The line between the values of the CEO and the values of the agency are—and should be—transparent and identical. If that line in values is distinctly obvious, or disparate, either the CEO has to adjust that organizational value, or find another organization to serve. This is a core distinction of innovative leadership: the leader's values directly inform the organization and must be closely aligned. Organizational values dictate the tone the CEO sets and people are held accountable to the expectations they have agreed to meet and the policies the board has set, all of which are aligned with the strategic direction the organization has selected.

The CEO plays the roles of both leader and manager to accomplish the important goal of guiding people to do the work of the agency and to serve the needs of the community. An example of managing is that each staff member has a job description and written expectations that he has acknowledged by signature, annual evaluations that do not include anything not previously discussed, and a professional development plan. An example of leading is ensuring that the management process and culture are aligned and evolving while continuing to meet the mission and uphold the organization's values.

Staff leadership requires fairness, the ability to set people up to succeed, to provide opportunities to learn from mistakes, and to celebrate victories. Successful CEOs never lose sight of the fact that staff is critical to the realization of goals as are all other factors.

Warren Buffet said, "In looking for people to hire, you look for three qualities: integrity, intelligence, and energy. And if they don't have the first, the other two will kill you." Another quality that we add to this list is organizational fit. There are many talented people who may not share your organizational values or who would not fit into your culture.

How a CEO hires and fires, trains, inspires, manages, rewards, evaluates, and promotes can benefit an organization and its goals, or be a detriment. Staff management is one of the most important aspects of leadership, and hiring is one of the most critical components of staff management.

It is not good enough for someone to be good at their job; they must also be moving the organization forward. In his book, *Good to Great,* Jim Collins uses the metaphor of a leader being the driver of a bus. "It is the leader's job to put the right person in the right seat. If in that seat, the person cannot perform, it's the leader's job to ask him to get off the bus."

Hiring is a process that takes into account the values of your agency, the skills and education required to do the job, the values and judgment of the candidates as evidenced by their answers to your questions and their references, the capacity of the applicant to fit on your team, and listening to your intuition. Intuition is that sixth sense that tells you if something isn't quite right even if you can't communicate why. Unfortunately, since gut instinct can't be explained, it allows for personal bias to come to come into play requiring the CEO to mitigate his own bias while still trusting his instinct. Every leader can tell the story of a time they hired someone even though their intuition told them not to. The story always ends with the person getting fired and the leader, finally, learning to trust his gut. Hiring right, after conducting a comprehensive search, leads to firing less often.

Good practices, planning, and training are a large part of managing risk. Risk management is easier than damage control. CEOs trained in risk management tend to filter major issues as potential newspaper headlines to be avoided and make decisions accordingly. It is very helpful to train staff on the variety of issues that can impact their jobs and the entire organization, as well as all the procedures and policies that apply.

One important area of staff development is teaching staff how to deal with crisis. Crisis management is a key component of risk management. A crisis management plan will direct the staff on what to do in a variety of dangerous situations while a crisis communication plan will inform who speaks for the organization and what staff should do when the media calls. Other documents, including personnel policies and standard operating procedures, will determine how staff is to behave in a range of situations. Plan and policy reviews, coupled with regular training, professional development opportunities, discussion of scenarios at staff meetings, feedback loops to address issues that have crisis potential, and accountability for action and inaction, all need to be combined to create the kind of innovative leadership that manages risk, rather than controls damage.

Program Development, Implementation, and Evaluation

CEOs are considered to be the subject matter expert in their field for their community. The art museum CEO is expected to be able to discuss at length the artists in her museum and how an artist's work contributed to the world of art. Youth development CEOs are expected to be able to discuss high school drop-out rates, the kindergarten readiness of five-year olds, youth and adolescent drug use, crime statistics, pregnancy rates of teens, and how their programs mitigate those numbers. Whatever the field, it is the CEO's role to paint the picture of how agency programs are filling the need, addressing the issues, and improving the community.

Programs are developed, often in conjunction with the constituents served, in an effort to address a gap or need in the community. Programs are reflective of the mission of the organization; that is, they are mission-driven. Mission-driven grant funding is a key component of resource development and has moved the needle for many nonprofit programs.

Unfortunately, programs are sometimes grant-driven and are not sustainable after the grant ends. The goal is to create programs to fill needs and generate long-term resources. Before a program is implemented, ensure it can be sustained. It is very difficult to maintain a good reputation if a needed program is introduced and later canceled due to lack of funds. Create sustainability plans for programs considered for introduction.

Programs must have a goal and a way to measure if that goal is met. For example, a school teacher is concerned that his students are not reading at grade level and wants to develop a tutoring program. After meeting with the parents and gaining their support, he goes to a local youth development agency to ask for their partnership. Then, he asks the PTA for a long-term commitment to support that partnership. Together they introduce a tutoring program and, in conjunction with the agency, assess its impact by the participants' grades as evidenced by report cards.

Measurements are gauged in terms of numbers or impact. Number measurement includes how many people were served, the hours of programming offered or the services provided. Number measurements, in grant terms, are called outputs. Outcome measurements tell if the program made an impact by working the way it was intended to work, and if the program made a meaningful difference in the client's life. Outcomes describe the overall impact. Together, outputs and outcomes offer a way to evaluate a program's effectiveness. Program assessment is an integral piece to ensure that the constituent's needs are being met in the most effective manner.

Collaboration and partnerships are also significant factors in programming. Most communities have a variety of organizations doing similar work and working toward similar goals. Invite those organizations to the table! Shared services and the exchange of best practices and resources make everyone stronger. Collaboration and partnering are also a way to attract more money and a more diverse array of programming for clients.

Policy, Plans, and Procedure Development

Policies, plans, and procedures allow a team to *do* what needs to be done, rather than spending time figuring out *what* needs to be done.

The board sets policy, often at the CEO's recommendation. The CEO sets operating procedures usually in consultation with the staff. The difference is akin to the difference between the rules, which are the procedures, and the law, which are the policies.

Board approved policies and codes include:

- Human Resources/Personnel
- Crisis Management and Communication
- By-laws/Code of Regulations
- Conflict of Interest
- Confidentiality
- Whistle Blowing

The majority of codes and policies have been previously mentioned. For those policies not specifically noted:

Human Resource/ Personnel	Applicable laws, policies, and procedures, employment status, pay periods, time off, hiring and orientation process, benefit structure and disciplinary process for an organization
Conflict of Interest	To ensure that decision makers and their families do not personally benefit from decisions they are making
Confidentiality	Confidentiality policies bind the staff to keep client and agency information private and not share any information they collect or process while fulfilling the duties of their position
Whistle Blowing	Sometimes included in an ethics policy, this is a mechanism that allows staff to report what they perceive to be an egregious violation

There is also a set of board-approved plans, many previously mentioned, that can help pave a successful path for your organization, as well as set some critical boundaries. Those plans include:

- Board Development
- Marketing
- Resource Development
- Strategic Plan
- Succession Plans

For plans not mentioned previously, please see the appendix for additional information.

The organization's values should be visible and obvious in every plan, policy, and procedure, and all systems. The CEO is ultimately responsible for implementing the policies, procedures, and plans—and holding people accountable to such plans. Innovative leadership requires alignment of values, culture, systems, and policies. If an organization purports to believe in the excellence of its people, for example, it cannot allow human resource systems that automatically promote staff or give across the board raises without merit. If no one is held accountable, then excellence is impossible.

Inspire and Engage

A large part of what CEOs do can be summed up in two words: inspire and engage.

CEOs inspire staff to believe in the mission and understand their roles in meeting the mission; they inspire the board and its committees to meet their goals and their governance responsibilities. CEOs inspire the community, donors, and volunteers, and engage each in their unique role in helping the organization to meet its mission.

CEOs are the face and the visionary of their organization. Everything the CEO does reflects on the organization. And the CEO, along with the senior staff and board, ensure the reputation of the agency. Because greater engagement creates greater organizations, CEOs also engage the community to believe in their vision. They engage the board to plan, and the staff to operationalize the plans created by the board. They inspire and engage everyone at every level to do more to help the organization meet its mission.

Inspiring and engaging, while incorporating and upholding organizational values, can be seen in each of the preceding sections and is an integral part of how innovative leaders lead.

Conclusion

> *Control is not leadership; management is not leadership; leadership is leadership. If you seek to lead, invest at least 50% of your time in leading yourself—your own purpose, ethics, principles, motivation, conduct. Invest at least 20% leading those with authority over you and 15% leading your peers.*
>
> — Dee Hock, founder and CEO Emeritus, Visa

The role of a nonprofit CEO is broad and diverse. When it's done well, it looks like nothing is being done at all! When it's done poorly, it's obvious to all. Most people only see the tip of the iceberg of the CEO role, and what they see will vary depending on their own role within an organization. The most successful CEOs hold people accountable, live their values, and align their organizations.

The following chapters outline the innovative leadership model in detail, providing a specific and tangible path for you to follow on your journey, and recount one CEO's experience in becoming an innovative leader.

CHAPTER 3
Step 1: Create a Compelling Vision of Your Future

The Innovative Leadership workbook is designed to provide a step-by-step process to support you in developing your own innovative leadership capacity. The fieldbook that serves as the foundation for this workbook has been tested with a broad range of clients as well as hundreds of working adults participating in an MBA program.

The comprehensiveness of these exercises coupled with reflection exercises will give you the insight into yourself and your organization needed to make substantive personal change. While this process appears linear, we have found that when leaders work through these steps, they often return to earlier parts of the process to clarify and sometimes refine their answers. The structure of our process will continue to challenge you to refine the work you have completed in prior exercises. First ideas are often good ones, yet when you work with this tool you will continually find insight. We encourage you to continue to test your ideas and feel comfortable circling back for further refinement.

These tools differ from many others by directing you through an exploration that takes into account your unique, individual experience while simultaneously considering the groups and organizations to which you belong.

The first step in starting your development process is cultivating a sense of clarity about your overall vision, which can also be summarized as your direction and aspirations. The intention behind your aspirations fuels both personal and professional goals, as well as a sense of meaning in your life. When your actions are aligned with your goals, they drive the impact you create in the world at large. As you move forward in the visioning process, we will guide you to begin thinking about individuals or groups who inspire or have a significant influence on you.

Simply put your vision and aspirations help you decide where best to invest your time and energy. Clarifying them helps you define a manner of contributing to the world that authentically honors who you are. Your vision and aspirations further help you clarify what you want to accomplish over time. You can select the time span that resonates for you, whether short-term—one to five years—or perhaps a longer-term time horizon, such as the span of your lifetime. After clarifying your own unique, personal vision, you will have the foundation for your ensuing change process. Knowing your vision and values creates the basis for your goals, and can help you align your behavior with your aspirations.

As part of the visioning process, it is important to consider the context of your leadership role, your organization or employer. If you are clear about your personal vision, you can evaluate where and how you fit within that organization. On the other hand, if your vision differs significantly from what you do and how you work, the additional information will guide you in finding a role that is a better fit (this transition may not happen in the short term). By knowing your vision and aspirations, you are equipped with information that helps you align the energy you invest with the work you do.

In addition to creating a well-defined vision, it is also important to be clear about your motivation. The combination of vision and desire is what will enable you to maximize your potential. Without sufficient desire, solid vision, and understanding of your current capabilities, you are likely to struggle when progress becomes difficult.

Tools and Exercises

The exercises will guide you in identifying what is most important to you. First, you will define your future, and from that vantage point, clarify your vision and values. You will then consider what you want to do professionally, as well as the type and extent of the impact you want to have on the world.

It is important to note that many people will participate in this exercise and still not have a clearly articulated vision—this is because defining personal vision requires a great deal of introspection for many people. While some people grow up knowing what they want to do for a living, for others identifying a vision is a process of gradual exploration and will take more time and energy than completing a single workbook exercise. You will likely refine your vision as you progress through later chapters in the workbook based on the information you learn about yourself. Because the visioning process is iterative in nature—a process of self-discovery—the exercises in this book will serve as the foundation for a longer process that may take considerably more time to complete. It will likely change as you gain experience and as your introspective process matures.

Define Personal Vision

Follow the steps defined below:

Step 1: Create a picture of your future. Imagine yourself at the end of your life. You are looking back and imagining what you have done and the results you have created.

- What is the thing you are most proud of?
- Did you have a family?
- What would your family say about you?
- What did you accomplish professionally?
- What would your friends say about you?

For the rest of this exercise, let that future person speak to you and help you set a path that will enable you to look back with pride and say things like, "I feel fulfilled and at peace. I lived my life well."

Step 2: Write a story. Now that you have that image of what you will accomplish, write a brief story about your successful life. Include details about the questions above. Make it a story of what you went through to accomplish each of the results for the questions you answered. What you are trying to create is a roadmap for your journey that gives you more insight into what you would want if you had the option to design your perfect life.

- Who helped you along the way?
- What did you enjoy about your daily life?
- Who was closest to you?
- What feelings did you have as you accomplished each milestone along the way?
- How did you mentor others and contribute to the success of others?
- What did you do to maintain your health?
- What role did spirituality or religion play in your journey?
- What job did you have?
- What role did material success play in your life?
- What type of person were you (kind, caring, driven, gracious)?

Step 3: Describe your personal vision. Given the story you have written and the qualities you demonstrated, write a two to five sentence life purpose statement—a statement that talks about your highest priorities in life and your inspirations. This statement should capture the essence of how you want to live your life and project yourself.

> *An example - My vision is to develop myself to my greatest capacity and help others develop and thrive in all aspects of their lives. I will live consciously and courageously, relate to others with love and compassion, and leave this world better for my contribution.*

Step 4: Expand and clarify your vision. If you are like most people, the choices you wrote are a mixture of selfless and self-centered elements. People sometimes ask, "Is it all right to want to be covered in jewels, or to own a luxury car?" Part of the purpose of this exercise is to suspend your judgment about what is "worth" desiring, and to ask instead which aspect of these visions is closest to your deepest desire. To find out, ask yourself the following questions about each element before going on to the next one: If I could have it now, would I take it?

Some elements of your vision don't make it past this question. Others pass the test conditionally: "Yes, I want it, but only if…" Others pass, but are further clarified in the process. As you complete this exercise, refine your vision to reflect any changes you want to make.

After defining and clarifying your vision, it is time to consider your personal values. The combination of these two exercises will help you create the foundation of what you want to accomplish and the core principles that guide your actions as you work toward your vision.

Checklist for Personal Values

Values are deeply held views of what we find worthwhile. They come from many sources: parents, religion, schools, peers, people we admire, and culture. Many go back to childhood; others are taken on as adults. Values help us define how we live our lives and accomplish our purpose.

Step 1: Define what you value most. From the list of values (both work and personal), select the ten that are most important to you as guides for how to behave, or as components of a valued way of life. Feel free to add any values of your own to this list.

PERSONAL VALUES CHECKLIST

▪ Achievement	▪ Intellectual status
▪ Advancement and promotion	▪ Leadership
▪ Adventure	▪ Location
▪ Arts	▪ Love
▪ Autonomy	▪ Loyalty
▪ Challenge	▪ Meaningful work
▪ Change and variety	▪ Money
▪ Community	▪ Nature
▪ Compassion	▪ Openness and honesty
▪ Competence	▪ Order (tranquility/stability)
▪ Competition	▪ Peace
▪ Cooperation	▪ Personal development/learning
▪ Creativity	▪ Pleasure
▪ Decisiveness	▪ Power and authority
▪ Democracy	▪ Privacy
▪ Economic security	▪ Public service
▪ Environmental stewardship	▪ Recognition
▪ Effectiveness	▪ Relationships
▪ Efficiency	▪ Religion
▪ Ethical living	▪ Reputation
▪ Excellence	▪ Security
▪ Expertise	▪ Self-respect
▪ Fame	▪ Serenity

PERSONAL VALUES CHECKLIST (CONT.)

- Fast living
- Fast-paced work
- Financial gain
- Freedom
- Friendships
- Having a family
- Health
- Helping other people
- Honesty
- Independence
- Influencing others
- Inner harmony
- Integrity
- Sophistication
- Spirituality
- Stability
- Status
- Time away from work
- Trust
- Truth
- Volunteering
- Wealth
- Wisdom
- Work quality
- Work under pressure
- Other: _____

Step 2: Elimination. Now that you have identified ten values, imagine that you are only permitted to have five. Which five would you give up? Cross them off. Now cross off another two to bring your list down to three.

Step 3: Integration. Take a look at the top three values on your list.

- How would your life be different if those values were prominent and practiced?

- What does each value mean, exactly? What are you expecting from yourself, even in bad times?

- Does the personal vision you've outlined reflect those values? If not, should your personal vision be expanded? Again, if not, are you prepared and willing to reconsider those values?

- Are you willing to create a life in which those values are paramount, and help an organization put those values into action?

Which one item on the list do you care most about?

Putting Vision into Action

After defining and clarifying your vision and values, the next step is to reflect on how to put them into action. You will consider the things you care about most as well as your innate talents and skills to determine what about your current life you would like to refine, or even change. You are probably passionate about specific interests or areas within your life; if you're really fortunate, you will have opportunities to participate in one or more of those areas.

The purpose of this exercise is to consider how best to incorporate your passions into how you make a living. You likely have passions that will always remain in the realm of hobbies; the main point of the exercise is to move closer to identifying your passions and expressing them in as many areas of life as possible.

In our experience, part of figuring out what you want to do is paying attention to what you find profoundly interesting. Those interests simply reveal themselves in the course of your daily interaction with peers and colleagues, and quite frequently at business functions. They are reflected in whatever you find yourself reading; they even display themselves in the context of more casual occasions, and are often seen in activities shared among friends.

This is the type of exercise that appears very simple on the surface, and may be something you revisit annually in order to refresh what is genuinely important for you. We find that revisiting allows you to nurture a sense of continual clarity about your direction. Iteration provides a mechanism for clarifying your direction as you grow and develop. With everything you try (false starts and all) you will discover a deeper truth about yourself that moves you closer to your most authentic passions. Some of those passions will be incorporated into your career; other passions help shape your personal life.

Exercise: Putting Vision into Action

Step 1: Identify your foundation. Answer the three questions below by compiling a list of responses to each.

- What are you passionate about? This will come from the prior exercise and should now be relatively concise.

- What meets your economic needs?

- What can you be great at?

Note - Your answers to these questions should reflect your values from the Personal Values Checklist.

Step 2: Review and identify overlap. Review your answers and identify the overlaps.

Step 3: Harvest the ideas. Based on the overlaps, do you see anything that might be incorporated in what you do or how you work? This could mean adding an additional service line to an existing business or allocating a portion of your work time to a project that is aligned with your values.

An example of this is a client who, based on significant reflection, learned he valued giving back to the community in a way that he was not doing at the time. He was the CEO of a technology firm. His passion was offering computer training for returning veterans; he maintained the job of CEO and added a community support function into his business. His passion for service to the community and professional skills afforded him the ability to follow his passion and still run a successful business. In the process of following his passion, he is building the workforce in his community and building his reputation as a civic leader and successful entrepreneur.

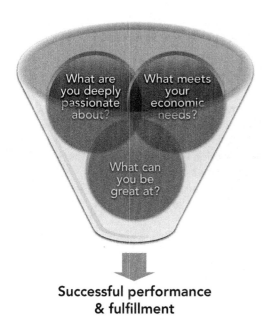

Successful performance & fulfillment

Vision-Based Actions

Innovative Leadership Reflection Questions

To help you develop your action plan, it is time to further clarify your direction using the reflection questions below. "What do I think/believe?" reflects your intentions. "What do I do?" questions reflect your actions. "What do we believe?" reflects the culture of your organization (i.e., work, school, community), and "How do we do this?" questions reflect systems and processes for your organization. This exercise is an opportunity to practice innovative leadership by considering your vision for yourself and how it will play out in the context of your life. You will define your intentions, actions, culture, and systems in a systematic manner.

Table 3-1 contains an exhaustive list of questions to appeal to a broad range of readers. You will likely find that a few of these questions best fit your own personal situation. Focus on the questions that seem the most relevant. We recommend you answer one to three questions from each category.

TABLE 3-1: QUESTIONS TO GUIDE THE LEADER AND ORGANIZATION

What do I think/believe?

- How do I see myself in the future? What trends do I see around me that impact this view? Have I considered how these trends impact the way I want to contribute?
- How does my view of myself impact me? Am I inspired by my vision? Terrified?
- How do I see myself within the larger environment? This can range from my family, the organization, to the global environment.
- After doing the exercises, what is my vision?
- After doing the exercises, what are my values? What do I stand for? What do I stand against?
- What are the connections between my business vision and my personal mission, passion, and economic goals?

What do I do?

- How do I gather input from key stakeholders to incorporate into my vision (family, business, self)?
- How do I research trends that will impact my industry so I can understand my future placement and how to navigate potential transitions in my industry?
- How do I synthesize competing goals and commitments to create a vision that works for me in the context of the communities I serve (family, friends, work, and community)?
- How do I develop my vision taking the greater economic conditions into account?
- What do I tell others about my vision? Do I have an "elevator speech"? Is it something I think is inspirational?

What do we believe?

- How does my personal vision fit within the larger context of my family, my community, my industry or my job?
- How do I create a shared belief that my vision will help the organization succeed within the larger community and also help the community succeed?
- What do we believe we stand for as an organization? How should we behave to accomplish what we stand for (guiding principles/values)? Do my values align with the organizational values?
- How do I reconcile differences between my values and those of my organization? How will these differences impact my ability to develop toward my vision and goals?

How do we do this?

- How do I monitor the organization's impact on my vision? How do I honor my vision when helping define/refine the organizational vision?
- What is our process for defining/refining changes to our shared vision for the organization and other systems I function within? What is our process for clarifying and documenting our values? How do I ensure that my values are aligned with our guiding principles?
- Who gives me feedback on their perspective of my progress? How often? What form would I like this feedback to take?
- What measures help me determine progress toward my vision and values? How do I track and report progress toward these goals? Is my behavior supporting the organizational goals? Are the organizational goals supporting my goals?

Introduction to Joey

At age 38, Joey accepted the CEO position of a youth organization that was in crisis. On a daily basis, she is involved in stabilizing the agency by raising its profile, building the programs, staff and board, and raising money and awareness. To help illustrate these reflection questions, we've included Joey's answers. We have tried to capture her internal thought process in these exercises in a way that is rare in a business context, but helpful for the purpose of personal development. We will now walk through answers to one or two questions from each section of Table 3-1. Simply follow along with Joey to answer the questions for yourself, or select the questions that fit your current situation.

What do I think/believe?

■ *How do I see myself in the future?*

I see myself as a person who can significantly contribute to this organization, grow its staff, board, and programs, and improve service to the clients we are privileged to serve. I also see myself as a community leader working not only to improve my own agency, but the community as a whole. I see myself raising my child in a supportive, healthy environment, and ensuring that he becomes a strong, healthy, happy, independent, and productive member of society. It feels discouraging as I look at all the challenges that face my organization today, but even so, I accept the challenge and commit to living and leading with integrity, honesty, and grace, and in grooming and guiding my staff and my family to realize their vision of themselves, and working beside them to create our vision of our future.

There are parts of my vision that I am not sharing here. They include my spiritual goals, relationship goals, and family goals. While I believe these are all critical to living a balanced and happy life, I am not sharing them in this journal because they are very personal to me.

■ *How does my view of myself impact me? Am I inspired by my vision? Terrified?*

I am inspired and a bit terrified. I have always thought all new challenges should be a 45/55 ratio between fear and excitement, and which emotion is greater depends on the day. Today, I feel inspired and the excitement holds greater sway: I am up for this challenge and will lead this organization to success! Along with the excitement is the fear that I will not succeed and that we will have to close the agency; there is also a wariness of the political capital I will have to spend to accomplish my goal, and the toll it will take on my health and my family.

I am aware of my faults and my strengths, and will try very hard to play to my strengths and work to improve in areas that I consider weaknesses. I am very hard on myself and think I should be perfect. I have had to learn that doing my best is as much as I can expect, but sometimes that isn't enough and I beat myself up for what others might consider small issues. I've never been great at asking for help, but I have also never faced the challenges that now stand before me. I will reach out to my peers when I am struggling with a situation, trust my instincts—while acknowledging my biases—and embody my values which I hope to instill as the organization's values.

■ *How do I see myself within the larger environment? This can range from my family, the organization, to the global environment?*

I see myself as a leader—of my agency, my community, and my family. Much of my contribution to the world happens through my organization. I work for a nonprofit that is changing the world for the children and families it serves. I want this organization to make a significant impact on our families, and also on how the larger community sees our families. If we are successful, we will impact people on all parts of the planet.

Beyond my work vision, I see myself as a person who tries to respect each individual with whom I come into contact. I believe my work and my kindness will impact the world in a positive way, yet I also acknowledge that leadership requires a certain edge and that the priorities of running a successful organization are occasionally in conflict with the preferences of the staff who serve that organization. As such, sometimes it is a very lonely job, which requires me all the more to have support and balance in all aspects of my life.

What do I do?

■ *How do I gather input from key stakeholders to incorporate into my vision (family, business, self)?*

I receive wonderful and positive feedback from my husband who is completely biased and very supportive. I continually seek, but don't always receive, external feedback from my colleagues, board, staff, friends, and constituents about what seems to be working and what isn't. The feedback I do receive comes in varying forms of recognition, frustration, or support. Of course, I continue to judge myself more harshly than others; sometimes people tell me about things I didn't see, wasn't aware of, or an impact I didn't intend. I'm grateful for those instances as they allow the chance for my own professional development. I believe in respectful dissent and try to encourage my team to hold each other and me accountable. It takes a certain self-confidence for staff to do that and I know that some never will possess that confidence. Still, I encourage it by checking in with them frequently about how they feel our relationship is going and directly asking for feedback on my leadership.

At this point in my life, I tend to be very introspective. I pay attention to my thoughts and feelings, and make time to think and reflect. This contemplation allows me to evaluate whether I am doing what I want to do and being the person I want to be. I am aware that many people believe they are following their inner guidance, yet have significant blind spots that interfere with clear, well-aligned actions. I check in with those I trust to make sure I stay grounded and realistic.

■ *How do I synthesize the competing goals and commitments to create a vision that works for me in the context of the communities I serve (family, friends, work, and community)?*

I work very hard at living and modeling a balanced life. I work during the hours of daycare which means I do not attend meetings at 7:30 in the morning. I am honest with people about why. I also leave work a bit early two days a week and announce that I am going to the gym. Nonprofit work is taxing and to be successful in this field we must achieve balance in our lives between work, family, friends, and personal time. If I am not healthy, none of the pieces in my life will be healthy. I have gone through a very deliberate process to create a plan for myself and my personal contributions, and to align my life to that plan. It is an ongoing process. I was raised with the understanding that we each have an obligation to work to make the world a better place and I try to do that.

I also know that no one is going to work harder than me on my own professional and personal development and that my utmost priority is to my child. Having a family requires an on-going realignment of priorities. I believe the more honest I can be about managing the competing priorities of my life, the better I can manage other people's expectations and stay aligned to my goal of living an authentic life. As I align my organization to the plans that govern it, I also have a plan for my own life and align and re-align my life to that plan.

I think of my life as a series of loops and redo-loops, all combining to help me achieve my vision. I always gather information, check that information against my own assessment and values, and gauge everything against my goal. I try out and try on new ideas, those that work I keep in my tool box; those that don't, I put down for now. As I try new things, I fail at some, yet use all the information I have gained—from successes, from failures, mistakes, and home runs—to pave my path and inform my journey.

I believe gratitude is an important force and I try to live and model gratitude. I never imagined I would be living the life I am, and every day I give thanks.

What do we believe?

■   *How does my personal vision fit within the larger context—my family, my community, my industry, my job?*

My vision is aligned with the larger nonprofit community. Many of us got into this field because of a deep commitment to social justice issues, and the work is something that is very personal and incredibly satisfying. I'm not sure my extended family understands the work, but they love me and support me anyway. My husband does, of course, and he supports and believes in my vision, which is also our vision. He and I share similar values which has been critical to the success of our marriage and our individual professional success. He is my biggest cheerleader, and as the job is sometimes very lonely, his support allows me to continue to keep my head in the game.

My personal vision is highly aligned with my organization. It is evolving, and the leadership team is very mindful of our collective culture and values and how they impact the organization. As it grows, we are taking more time to ensure that we listen to the values and concerns of others, and integrate them into the organizational systems. We find that people of similar values are attracted to our organization and those who differ significantly simply are not. As we are aware of our values and seek those with similar values to join our team, our organization has continued to be aligned and on point which has greatly contributed to our success.

■ *What do we believe we stand for as an organization? What do we believe about how we should behave to accomplish what we stand for (guiding principles/values)? Do my values align with those organizational values?*

We stand for social justice, empathy, personal accountability, respect, and empowerment, and try to instill those values in the children we serve. Our mission and our values are infused throughout our programming, our buildings, and our literature. We are consistent in how people are held accountable and we each work to live those values. That means we treat our clients and everyone with respect, that there are myriad voices at the table when decisions are being made, and our systems support rather than conflict with those values. As we are a nonprofit, it is also visible in how we speak to and about the children we serve and in how they speak to each other and about themselves.

How do we do this?

■ *Who gives me feedback on their perspective of my progress? How often? What form would I like this feedback to take?*

Getting feedback as a nonprofit CEO is difficult. Board members and community leaders consistently show their appreciation, which I value. Staff members show their respect, and sometimes their frustration. Yet, concrete, specific feedback is hard to come by. I have learned to ask for it directly, adding that I cannot grow as a professional unless I am regularly evaluated and receive ongoing feedback. My coach has really assisted me in this, as coaching sessions are the one place that I can speak freely without fear of being judged.

There are, of course, measurement tools that provide feedback, impact measurements for the organization, achievement of the strategic plan, and a 360° assessment tool (providing feedback from my board and my staff) that measures individual performance and organizational culture.

■ *What measures help me determine progress toward my vision and values? How do I track and report progress against these goals? Is my behavior supporting the organizational goals? Are the organizational goals supporting my goals?*

I am consistently checking in with myself to see if I am aligned with my goals and with my organization's goals. I do a personal assessment each spring to decide if my vision and values should be refined. I also look at the organization's impact goals and take stock of the previous year to celebrate our successes and review what I, personally, could have done differently to better embody my values and the organization's values.

Each spring, we have a full organizational review, with the board and staff, to re-align, revise or recommit to our plan, our values, and our mission. It includes reviewing each system as it compares to best practices, and a review of each person's expectations and professional development goals of the past year and for the upcoming year. We conclude with setting new programmatic and organizational goals for the new year and defining each person's role in meeting those goals.

Your Process of Creating a Compelling Vision

Now that you have read Joey's personal narratives, it is time to complete the exercises and answer the questions for yourself. We encourage you to complete all of the exercises; these exercises establish a strong foundation for your personal vision, values, and course of action; so exercise patience and give yourself time to explore your hopes and dreams as authentically as possible. You will know you've completed this step and are ready to move to the next when you feel you have created a vision and set of values that truly inspire you.

Throughout this chapter, we have discussed exercises that will help you clarify your life direction and create a compelling vision for your own life and work. The next chapter focuses on assessing where you are right now in your career and personal development.

Define personal vision

What do I think/believe?

What do I do?

What do we believe?

How do we do this?

CHAPTER 4
Step 2: Analyze Your Situation and Strengths

Now that you have developed (or refined) your vision, it is time to examine your strengths and development opportunities. This step will help you refine and clarify those strengths and weaknesses using standard assessment tools. You will then decide which areas you would like to improve by building on what you already do well and addressing weaknesses. We recommend using a general guideline that focuses 80% of your effort on building your existing strengths and 20% on addressing weaker areas. Though this a general approximation, the 80/20 rule is a directional one stemming from the belief that you are already successful and have simply taken the opportunity to further advance and refine your capabilities. If you find serious deficiencies, those deficiencies can be best addressed by other leadership books and resources.

It is important to combine your vision with a firm understanding of your current performance, abilities, and personality type. The data will help you become more aware of your strengths and weaknesses, and also clarify how others see you. The combination of information will help you determine the gap between your current state (based on assessment data) and your vision.

It is important to note that many people have a higher capacity than they are able to use at work. This could be caused by working in a job that does not use your full abilities. When you begin taking assessments, it will be important to get information from a broad range of sources to ensure you have a clear and accurate picture of your true capacity.

Assessment Tools

One of the primary ways to help you understand your current development and performance is using a combination of assessments to measure your current skills and abilities, along with your personality style and developmental perspective. This should allow you to identify the gap between your present state and what you need to fulfill your vision.

There are several good assessments available. The tools we suggest have been used extensively with our clients and are recommended with a high degree of confidence. We find that each provides vital information in helping to convey a comprehensive picture of strengths, weaknesses, and opportunities. These assessments are aligned with the five elements of innovative leadership

Leadership Behaviors

Situational Analysis

Resilience

Developmental Perspective

Leader Type

discussed in chapter one. Some are expensive and require a skilled coach to interpret them; this option is not practical for everyone. Metcalf & Associates has created a free online assessment that does not replace the detailed assessments recommended below, but does offer a high-level view of your innovative leadership and can indicate key areas of focus. It can be accessed by going to http://www.metcalf-associates.com/innovative-leadership-assessment.html.

The tools we use to help develop innovative leaders are:

■ **Leader Type Assessment using the Enneagram**

We recommend using the Enneagram first and foremost to <u>discover your own personality type</u> and, as appropriate, to determine the types of those with whom you interact. The Enneagram is used for personal growth, relationships, therapy, and in the business world as an indicator of an individual's primary personality type. The <u>*Riso-Hudson Enneagram Type Indicator*</u> (version 2.5) provides a reliable, <u>independently scientifically validated</u> tool for that purpose. Finding your type is not the final goal, but merely the starting place for working with our system, and embarking on a fascinating and rewarding journey of self-reflection.

The Enneagram helps you to see your *own* personality dynamics more clearly. Once you are aware of the importance of personality types, you see that your own style is not equally effective with everyone. One of the Enneagram's most useful lessons is how to move from a style of interacting in which others are expected to mold themselves to your way of thinking and values to a more flexible style in which you act from an awareness of the strengths and potential contributions of others. By doing so, you help others become more effective themselves—and as a result, harmony, productivity, and satisfaction are likely to increase. The Enneagram is an inexpensive assessment that is available online and does not require a certified coach to interpret (source: www.enneagraminstitute.com/practical.asp).

■ **Developmental Perspective**

We recommend the Maturity Assessment Profile (MAP) to evaluate developmental perspective. Dr. Susanne Cook-Greuter developed this assessment to describe developmental perspectives as part of her Ph.D. at Harvard University. It is widely considered one of the most rigorously validated, reliable, and advanced assessment tools used to evaluate adult leadership development. Participants taking the assessment complete thirty-six sentence stems about various topics. The freeform response format allows test takers to provide a wide range of information, which gives the scorer ample data to evaluate varying developmental features along three main lines: cognitive complexity, emotional affect, and behavioral. The combination of the three allows the scorer to determine the action logic or how people tend to reason and respond to life. It is critical for you to be completely open and honest when taking this assessment in order for there to be sufficient data to provide an accurate score. The MAP assessment is available through Pacific Integral (www.pacificintegral.com) or Susanne Cook-Greuter (www.cook-greuter.com). This assessment requires a coach to interpret the data and comes with a detailed report explaining the developmental levels and the perspectives each offers.

Resilience Assessment

Metcalf & Associates created a basic tool to help you assess your attitudes and practices that help support resilience, and identify areas where you can further build your capacity. It is based on fundamental stress management research including the characteristics that support "stress hardiness," a concept pioneered by Suzanne Kobasa. This assessment can be found at http://www.metcalf-associates.com/resilience-assessment-tool.html.

The Leadership Circle Profile (LCP) Competency Based 360° assessment

This tool looks specifically at a set of well-researched leadership behaviors as key levers to drive success.

It is important for a leader to have an accurate view of what others see to be able to make appropriate changes and gauge the impact of these changes. This tool not only allows you to identify possible behavioral changes, it can also help you improve your self-awareness by specifically understanding how others see you. It is this ability to see what others see that will allow you to target your behavioral changes and fine-tune your effectiveness. The Leadership Circle is available at www.theleadershipcircle.com and requires a certified coach to administer and provide feedback.

How others perceive you is, in part, based on their own values and overall view of the world. Interpreting that data can be just as much an art as scientific inference. Rather than taking such feedback at face value, we suggest trying to understand those evaluations as well as the culture of the organization. For example, if an individual is very results-oriented in a culture that prefers collaboration, that individual may be perceived as having a negative disposition—controlling, driven, and autocratic. Another organization with a culture that is more aligned with a results-driven approach may perceive that very same individual as being extremely positive—achieves results, vision-focused, and system-oriented. Part of understanding development and effectiveness is finding the organization aligned with your leadership style, as well as a culture that can support your potential to grow.

The Leadership Agility 360 degree Assessment assesses a manager's level of agility within key behavioral arenas.

The **Leadership Agility 360** (LA360) is based on the research underlying the award-winning book, *Leadership Agility: Five Levels of Mastery for Anticipating and Initiating Change* by William B. Joiner and Stephen A. Josephs. This research shows that managers have the potential to grow through a series of "leadership agility levels" that make them increasingly effective in leading change, leading teams, and engaging in pivotal conversations.

The Leadership Circle Profile and Leadership Agility 360 assessments complement one another. Each of the three agility levels included in this assessment is the <u>behavioral embodiment</u> of a well-documented stages of development referenced in the developmental perspective section above and measured by the MAP. They are:

- **Expert:** Using one's technical and functional expertise to make tactical organizational improvements, supervise direct reports, identify and solve key problems, and sell these solutions to others.

- **Achiever:** Setting clear organizational objectives, leading strategic change, motivating and orchestrating team performance, working across boundaries, and stepping up to challenging conversations.

- **Catalyst (Individualist):** Leading transformative change that develops agile, sustainable organizations and highly-engaged teams; and collaborating with others to develop creative, high-leverage solutions to thorny organizational issues. Currently, only about 5% of managers act with consistency at this level, yet, of the three, this agility level is one of the most effective in navigating today's increasingly complex and rapidly changing environment.

The **LA360** is the only behavioral feedback assessment designed to identify specifically where managers are in this developmental process.

It is very helpful to take multiple assessments during the same period of time to paint a more complete and accurate picture of who you are as a leader. For example, the Enneagram shows your personality type; the MAP shows your ability to take multiple perspectives associated with levels of development; and the LCP shows how you are perceived by others, as well as how you see yourself. The combined or integrated assessment allows you to better understand your innate skills and abilities as well as your opportunities. This comprehensive information allows you to determine how you fit within your organization. Keep in mind that interpreting the data from these and other assessments often requires specialized expertise; we strongly recommend working with a certified coach. Similar to getting medical tests, the potential value of the information is only realized with proper translation. Having a coach interpret the series of assessments as the foundation for your development plan can significantly increase your success, since you will know exactly where to focus your efforts.

Now that we have presented four different types of assessments, you have the opportunity to select the ones you are moved to take and consider how best to utilize the results.

Future Projections

We find that reading futurist publications in specific industries is helpful. The role of the futurist is to evaluate current trends and build possible scenarios for how the future might unfold. By building on our capacities for leadership, we can use these scenarios as part of our planning process to provide insight into overall societal trends, ensure we are well prepared for the potential impact of ever-changing business conditions, and suggest imminent scenarios that help you navigate those trends effectively.

There are several organizations providing very effective views into the future. One that we regularly reference is The Arlington Institute (TAI), founded in 1989 by futurist John L. Petersen. It is a nonprofit research institute that specializes in thinking about global futures and creating conditions to influence rapid, positive change. They encourage systemic, non-linear approaches to planning and believe that effective thinking about the future is enhanced by applying emerging technology. TAI strives to be an effective agent of advancement by creating intellectual frameworks and toolsets for understanding the transition in which we are living.

Tools and Exercises

Now that you have reviewed the tools and taken some or all of the assessments, it is time to synthesize what you have learned about yourself through a Strengths, Weaknesses, Opportunities, and Threats worksheet (SWOT) and through a series of reflection questions. For the SWOT analysis, please complete the worksheet below.

TABLE 4-1: SWOT ANALYSIS	
Strengths What sets you apart from most other people?	**Opportunities** What opportunities are open to those who have these strengths?
Weaknesses What do you need to improve?	**Threats** Do you have weaknesses that need to be addressed before you can move forward? Do any pose an immediate threat like losing your job?

Joey's Development Journey Continued

Joey will now walk through her worksheets and journal entries for analyzing her situation and strengths.

JOEY'S SWOT WORKSHEET ANSWERS	
Strengths What sets you apart from most other people? - Extensive nonprofit leadership experience - Experience in youth and family services - History of social justice work - Master's degree - I am good at my work and I love what I do - Comfortable addressing conflict	**Opportunities** What opportunities are open to those who have these strengths? - Run a larger organization that makes a greater impact on the world - Teach, mentor, and develop others - Continue to grow as a leader
Weaknesses What do you need to improve? - Frustration with others who are low performers or cannot see the big picture - Direct communicator, which sometimes puts people off - Sense of urgency that is occasionally unwarranted - Quest for perfection	**Threats** Do you have weaknesses that need to be addressed before you can move forward? Do any pose an immediate threat to you, such as losing your job? - No immediate threats, but certainly areas I would like to improve - Building additional emotional calm and the ability to put challenges into a longer-term perspective will help - Realizing that many of the frustrations in life are important lessons for me, and that in some cases I just need to let others move at their own pace

Innovative Leadership Reflection Questions

To help you develop your action plan, it is time to further clarify your direction using reflection questions. The questions for "What do I think/believe?" reflect your intentions. "What do I do?" questions reflect your actions. The questions "What do we believe?" reflect the culture of your organization (i.e. work, school, community), and "How do we do this?" questions reflect systems and processes for your organization. This exercise is an opportunity to practice innovative leadership by considering your vision for yourself and how it will play out in the context of your life. You will define your intentions, actions, culture, and systems in a systematic manner.

Table 4-2 contains an exhaustive list of questions to appeal to a broad range of readers. Find a few that fit your own personal situation; focus on the questions that seem the most relevant. We recommend you answer one to three questions from each category.

TABLE 4-2: REFLECTION QUESTIONS

What do I think/believe?

- Given the direction the world is unfolding, how do you believe you are positioned to be a leader in the future?

- Are you able to balance professional and personal commitments? How does your leadership style impact your ability to meet your overall life goals?

- How has your leadership style contributed to the organization's success? Have you done things that did not produce the results you had hoped? How would you change to produce different results?

- How would you like to impact the people who work for you? Have they grown and met their career goals while working for you? What have they contributed to the organization while working for you?

What do I do?

- How do you play to your strengths?

- How do you mitigate the threats?

- How do you take advantage of opportunities?

- How do you compensate for weaknesses?

- What assessments are you taking to gather objective data about your performance? This could include performance appraisals, developmental assessments, 360° feedback, or informal feedback from multiple sources.

- How do you appropriately respond to your personal sense of urgency while supporting organizational objectives?

- What messages do you convey that use emotion, external expert sources, and sense of clarity to demonstrate urgency?

- How do you communicate your personal changes and your sense of urgency to those around you who may be impacted?

What do we believe?

- Notice the various people and groups in your life (family, colleagues, boss, community, friends, etc.) and what they report as "urgent."

- Anticipate how they will interpret your change. How will they talk about it? Specifically for your organization, how will the changes you aspire to make impact your constituents?

- Determine how your sense of urgency connects with the group's sense of urgency based on its priorities, goals, and pain points.

- How does the culture of your support system impact your beliefs about yourself and about leadership? Would these beliefs change if you changed who you spent time with?

- Based on developmental perspectives, where is the cultural center of gravity in your support system? How are people with more open perspectives perceived?

- What are the cultural barriers to you changing? What are the cultural enablers? Will your changes be aligned with the organizational culture? Will they send a message that you do not value the culture?

> **How do we do this?**
>
> - Which systems and processes are enablers and barriers that will impact my development?
>
> - Which processes and measures alert us to urgency in our system that we need to tend to? What are the early warning signs?
>
> - Which processes measure your progress? Are you progressing as measured by criteria that will increase your professional effectiveness? Are you progressing against your personal standards? How will your support system or organization reward or punish your changes based on the measures?
>
> - Do the measures indicate a sense of urgency to you that support focusing on development?

Joey's Reflection Responses

We will now walk through Joey's answers to one or two questions from each section of Table 4-2. Simply follow along with Joey to answer the questions for yourself, or select questions that fit your current situation.

What do I think/believe?

- *Given the direction the world is unfolding, how do you believe you are positioned to be a leader in the future?*

  The nonprofit world is ever changing and refining itself. I believe I am at the forefront of that refinement, leading our community toward collaboration between various youth organizations—a collaboration which has not yet happened. Additionally, as a large majority of nonprofit leaders will be retiring in the coming years, I am positioning myself to be a future leader of a larger organization, while steering my current organization toward better systems and insured sustainability. Given the information in my SWOT analysis, I believe I am well positioned.

- *How has your leadership style contributed to the organization's success? Have you done things that did not produce the results you had hoped for? How would you change to produce different results?*

  My leadership and my direct communication style have allowed us to quickly address an immediate issue and reorganize the agency to ensure its continued presence in our community. Unfortunately, it also alienated some families who were unhappy with the changes and some staff who did not embrace the change, which means either I did not explain it enough or well enough, or they did not agree with my decisions. I will need to work to re-engage those constituents.

■ *How satisfied are you with your performance?*

Satisfied isn't a goal, or maybe it isn't enough of a goal for me. Am I moving the needle? Is my agency stronger? Are my kids impacted? Is my family healthy? Am I living an authentic life? I am creating a life that can answer yes to all of the preceding questions and for that to happen, I need to inspire my team and my family to greatness!

What do I do?

■ *How do you take advantage of opportunities?*

To take advantage of the opportunities, I will need to create buy-in for my vision. That means that rather than moving into that model immediately, which is my preference, I will have to spend the necessary time explaining the changes I would like to implement, receiving feedback on these changes, and realigning those changes based on feedback. Sometimes we will receive feedback that I do not agree with but can live with, and depending on the circumstances, I will find a way to do that. However, if the feedback greatly changes the direction, I will find a way to avoid the group's input from derailing us, yet will continue to create opportunities for people to join the movement toward the change initiative I am leading. If I do this well, not only will it greatly improve the organization, but will establish me as a leader in my field and my community.

■ *How do you communicate your personal changes and your sense of urgency to those around you who may be impacted?*

To continue to excel in my role, I want to improve the way I respond to things that I perceive as having a sense of urgency; essentially, I want to make sure there is an actual sense of urgency and not one I created. I also want to listen better and make sure I am hearing what others are saying. I believe that to grow in this area, I need to develop skills to be more aware of others' reactions to my decisions. The CEO role requires me to move quickly, but that speed can't be at the expense of my team.

■ *What messages do you convey that use emotion, external expert sources, and sense of clarity to demonstrate urgency?*

I talk about what I learned from the assessment and what I am doing about it. I also ask others for constructive feedback on a regular basis. I realize that as a leader, this request is a tough one and I want others to see that I am willing to make personal changes to become more effective. When I ask them to do the same, they will know that I am not asking any more of them than what I ask of myself.

What do we believe?

◪ *Anticipate how they will interpret your change. How will they talk about it? Specifically for your organization, how will the changes you aspire to make impact your constituents?*

My organization, like many others, has a variety of constituents that have different relationships with the organization, including, staff, board, donors, clients, families, partner agencies, and the larger community. As I mentioned previously, some of the families and staff were frustrated and angry by the initial changes. Some of those changes were dictated by money and some of the changes were to address a lack of systems, which was where we started our change management process. Some of the staff and parents didn't like it—they felt it was too much too fast—yet it had to be done. The money piece was easier to justify. There simply was not the money to continue the program as it had been operating, and, as a leader, my job is to ensure the future of the organization. I then needed to re-engage the staff that remained and the families toward buying into my vision. The provision of safer programs, a better environment, and better systems greatly assisted me toward that effort. The board, donors, partner agencies, and community were frustrated by the very thing—the lack of systems—that the staff and families liked and were immediately enthused by the new vision and willing to help me achieve change.

How do we do this?

◪ *What processes measure your progress? Are you progressing as measured by criteria that will increase your professional effectiveness?*

Are you progressing against your personal standards? How will your support system or organization reward or punish your changes based on the measures? I have annual expectations to meet, as do all members of our team. Our progress is measured against those expectations as well as the impact, revenue, and system goals for our agency. Our organization provides an internally developed abridged version of the 360 assessment for all leaders. As I believe that the organization is only as successful as our leadership, this is a great driver for me and for us. I use the results of the 360 assessment as the beginning of a dialogue between my team and me to discuss how we can work together more effectively as a unit and how I can better assist them to meet their professional goals.

◪ *What processes and measures alert us to urgency in our system that we need to tend to? What are the early warning signs?*

The earliest warning sign is a crisis or potential crisis in the program. It not only tells me that we missed a training opportunity, but that we put a child—and, consequently, our organization—in danger. Any time something like that occurs, we add it to the training module for the next training. It is critical to all that we learn from our mistakes to ensure they do not happen again. I also hope that this creates a culture of re-do loops. None of us are perfect and, as such, need to create opportunities to learn from our mistakes to ensure they are not repeated. Life is about making new mistakes.

Your Process of Evaluating Your Situation and Strengths

Now that you have followed Joey's responses, it is time to complete the worksheets. Based on your assessment results, if you have not done so already, complete the SWOT analysis in Table 4-1 and answer one to three questions from each section in Table 3-2 for yourself. By internalizing your strengths and opportunities, you can identify the gaps that, when filled, will help you to accomplish your vision. Understanding your weaknesses will also help you know what to avoid, what to improve, and what personal feedback to request from people skilled in those areas.

We encourage you to complete all of the exercises, taking your time and giving proper attention to gathering input from several different sources. When you have a clear picture of your strengths and opportunities, you will be ready to move to the next step. You may now find that you have a different or clearer perception about where you excel, and how those areas can complement your vision.

This chapter helped you clarify your strengths and weaknesses as a foundation for your personal transformation journey. Bear in mind that you are creating your own story through this process. The next chapter focuses on the framework for creating a development plan that will allow you to close the gap between your vision and where you are today.

Resources

- **Enneagram:** www.enneagraminstitute.com

- **Mature Adult Profile Assessment (MAP):** www.pacificintegral.com

- **The Leadership Circle 360° Assessment:** www.theleadershipcircle.com

- **Resilience Assessment:** www.metcalf-associates.com

- **Overall Innovative Leadership Assessment:** www.metcalf-associates.com

- **Susanne Cook-Greuter research:** www.cook-greuter.com

- **Leadership Agility 360:** www.changewise.biz

What do I think/believe?

What do I do?

What do we believe?

How do we do this?

How do we do this?

CHAPTER 5

Step 3: Plan Your Journey

When you have a solid plan for your development journey, you begin investing your time and energy based on your vision, your strengths and weaknesses, and your development goals. In order to stay motivated, it is important to experience a sense of measurable growth. Tangible results are especially crucial to implementing change, and demonstrating progress is naturally part of the expectation. An example is: If my boss wants me to show that I am a good leader before he will promote me, I need to show that I am "good" as measured by the boss's criteria. So, in this case, I would want to understand the criteria as well as know what the boss values, and build a plan that allows me to show those results. On the other hand, if I am developing for my own personal growth, I may not be as concerned about showing results to others, but will still want to feel I am making progress.

As you can imagine, some results will take longer than others to manifest. Our experience with clients has shown that leaders can certainly make quick progress in some areas, but others can take years.

Your life situation will also impact your development. For example, a leader may be a great provider for his family, and this is a core value he holds. He might create meaningful results that help cultivate developmental growth by focusing on specific behaviors that will promote his well-being and success. In other words, he may simply experience a sense of progress ranging from a greater feeling of calm, clearer thinking, and better relationships with colleagues which will lead to better performance. He may also see measured results quantitatively using a 360° assessment (gaining feedback from several stakeholder groups at multiple levels within the organization including boss, peers, and subordinates) showing significant improvements in key leadership-related qualities. Another leader who wants to have a greater impact on the world may have an entirely different development focus and plan.

Consider the value of investing your energy in this journey as a way to foster meaningful change for the people closest to you. If you know, for example, that you have specific behaviors that are particularly difficult for your boss, an important colleague, or a loved one, you may want to prioritize those areas for improvement.

Options Development Plan Focus

To accomplish your vision, you may benefit from one or all of the following three developmental focuses:

- **Becoming more effective; developing new skills and/or behaviors** – Changing behaviors and building skills that will significantly impact performance, as measured by observed behavioral change. As you advance in your job responsibilities and/or as the organizational environment changes, you will continually need to build new skills. These can range from an understanding of how to leverage social media to promote your organization to building a board. In this category, the focus is on skills that can be developed through training programs.

- **Building on your current strengths** – Development can take the form of focusing on enhancing current strengths. It can also focus on important behaviors that adversely impact success. Again, we recommend focusing 80% of your effort toward building on your passions and the other 20% toward shoring up your deficiencies. This is a general recommendation; it is important to remember that your specific situation and needs will be clear indicators of what changes are required for your continued growth and success.

- **Minimizing your weaknesses** – In the Strengths, Weaknesses, Opportunities, and Threats (SWOT) analysis, you may have identified some behaviors that impede further growth. These may have been behaviors that made you successful in your current development (sometimes referred to as overused strengths). Even so, part of your development is examining the events and behaviors that got you here and understanding which interfere with your success as defined by your vision. For example, you may identify yourself as someone who is on top of every task. As your responsibilities grow, you will delegate more, but you may still feel uncomfortable with your lack of knowledge of the details. Trying to manage the details to the level that made you successful will become a weakness as you move up. It is important to tend to these behavioral changes as part of your plan. The challenge here may be shifting the focus away from daily details toward strategic thinking and expanding your ability beyond one or a few core strengths to develop several additional capabilities.

As you begin building your capacity, you may want to consider two distinct, yet essential, areas, external capacity and internal capacity. Though the research emphasizing the importance of both is compelling, most of our formal training still focuses on hard skills (external capabilities). This exclusive emphasis leaves many leaders ill-prepared for, and in some cases uninformed about, the importance of internal capacity, such as emotional intelligence and interpersonal skills. Research among Fortune 500 companies at Stanford University showed that 90% of those who failed as leaders did so because they lacked the interpersonal skills that are a critical component of emotional intelligence. This is confirmed by research conducted by the Center for Creative Leadership finding that poor interpersonal skills are a leading cause of derailment from executive-level positions. These terms are defined as:

- **External capacity (hard skills)** – Skills and behaviors associated with professional success. This is where most professional development efforts have been focused.

- **Internal capacity** – Includes intention, world view, purpose, vision, values, cultural norms, emotional stability, resilience, a sense of being grounded, overall personal well-being, intuition, balanced perspective, and attitude, and serves as the foundation for you to accomplish your deepest aspirations. Internal capacity is also required to move on to later stages of development.

In most organizations, the vast majority of development efforts focus on hard skills (including advanced degrees and certification programs), and thus, many leaders need to balance them by explicitly exercising internal capacity. To further describe this process, we use the term mastery, which simply means the capacity to not only produce results, but also to master the principles underlying those results. In other words, as a master, you can deliver results comfortably due to the internal capacity behind your skills and judgment.

Personal mastery involves enhancing your internal capacity to support the skills you have acquired while also removing barriers to your success. To help you achieve personal mastery, we recommend you enrich your ongoing development plan and personal practices (activities we repeat until we master them, like our golf swing).

There are some important factors to consider when creating your plan. First, just as in physical training, you will get more leverage if you cross-train or develop several areas at the same time. According to Ken Wilber (AQAL Framework), there are benefits to cross-training beyond simply focusing on one area. For example, people who both lift weights and meditate tend to make greater improvements in both areas than those who do one or the other. Evidence suggests that a combination of activities from different parts of our lives complement one another. This is quite true in the leadership arena as well.

A comprehensive plan will take into consideration each of the dimensions that are foundational to the human experience: physical, emotional, mental, and spiritual (people not comfortable with the term *spiritual* can substitute *altruistic* or *purpose*). If any of these elements are neglected, you are likely to find it will adversely impact your success in other areas over the long term.

There are standard programs designed to help this process. One of the programs we suggest is Integral Transformative Practice (ITP), developed by Michael Murphy and George Leonard. This practice involves a strong cross-training routine. Nine commitments form the essential building blocks of the ITP program. They create the roadmap for practitioners to follow to realize their potential through the cross-training of body, mind, heart, and soul. The commitments include aerobic exercise, mindful eating, strength training, staying emotionally current, a service component, and the ITP Kata, which is a 40-minute series involving movements derived from yoga and Aikido, deep relaxation techniques, imagery, affirmations, and meditation. ITP is a long-term program for realizing the potential of body (exercise), mind (reading, discussion), heart (staying emotionally current, community), and soul (meditation, affirmations). Joining a local ITP group can augment a strong individual practice.

Tools and Exercises

The range of tools is quite broad, so it is important to select something that feels safe and consistent with your values. The goal is to create a plan that you can follow and stick with to accomplish your goals. To help you get started, we put suggestions in Table 5-1. While several items fall within multiple categories, we attempted to classify them to be as mutually exclusive as possible. Some activities will provide benefits across several categories. An example of this is meditation, as it can help you manage your negative thinking, improve focus, balance emotions, and improve decision-making capacity.

Healthy development encompasses work in all areas. The practices you choose may evolve, and your practice may also fluctuate based on other life demands. We encourage you to maintain as much consistency as possible. Just as the benefit of exercise increases when you hit a specific frequency and duration, the same will be true for leadership development practices. The more you invest, the better your results will be.

TABLE 5-1: RECOMMENDATIONS FOR INTERNAL AND EXTERNAL CAPACITY BUILDING - ACTIVITIES TO CONSIDER INCORPORATING INTO PLAN

What activities can I do to impact my internal capacity (what I think and believe)?

- Spirit
  - Define vision
  - Define values
  - Pray
  - Participate in religious practices
  - Religious study
  - Seek spiritual counseling
  - Seek a spiritual teacher
  - Visualize goals
  - Become socially active – volunteer
- Ethics
  - Create guiding principles or values
  - Pay attention to ethics around you
  - Address situations you find unethical
  - Read and learn about ethics

- Emotions (Emotional Quotient)
  - Meditate
  - Seek therapy
  - Practice HeartMath techniques
  - Practice shadow exercises - the ability to find in yourself the things you find frustrating in others and address them as growth opportunities
  - Keep a journal
  - Seek coaching
  - Maintain strong friendships

What activities can I do to impact my external capacity?

- Body
  - Exercise
  - Yoga
  - Relaxation
  - Weight lifting
  - Mindful eating / healthy diet
  - Sufficient sleep
- Cross Training
  - Integral Transformative Practice (yoga, aikido, relaxation, visualization, meditation)
  - Reflection practices (do-reflect-learn)

- Mind
  - Read
  - Study
  - Attend lectures and discussion groups
  - Attend school
  - Perspective-taking exercises
  - Take stretch assignments
  - Volunteer for opportunities to build skills (charity work)
  - Manage polarities
  - Action inquiry
  - Mindfulness-Based Stress reduction

What activities can I do that impact us as a group (what we think/believe)?

- Review the list above, and determine which activities can be completed in a group. What groups do I participate in, and do they have similar values?

- Develop a mission and values as a family. You may choose to set family meditation time or gym time to promote a family sense of focus and well-being. Many families share religious traditions and find that they provide a solid foundation and a shared set of values

What structures and/or groups will help? What groups or programs do I participate in?

- Family activities could include how we eat, our exercise routines, our family reading time, our church or spiritual practice, and our volunteer activities

- Friend/social activities include what I do with my friends that support and that hinder my development, such as exercise groups, emotional support, honest and accurate feedback, and dialogue practices

- Work events and support, including yoga classes, weight management support, fitness classes, insurance discounts for fitness, and smoking cessation programs

- Practice groups for development, such as Integral Transformative Practice, meditation, and church

- Study groups

- Formal education programs

- Informal education programs

- Fitness groups and programs, such as running clubs, ski clubs, exercise groups, and gym memberships

The following is a development plan template designed to help you create a plan that allows you achieve your goals. This table focuses mainly on identifying opportunities and the intentions behind your desire to change.

	TABLE 5-2: SKILL/BEHAVIOR DEVELOPMENT WORKSHEET Evaluate and Select Skill/Behavioral Change Priorities – Worksheet	
Key Actions	**Detailed Action Planning**	**Behavior 1**
Select behaviors	Which behaviors do I want to improve or change? Which behaviors do I perform well that I would like to enhance?	
What are the consequences of this behavior?	What will happen if I continue to demonstrate this behavior in the future? How will my service recipients be impacted? How will my career be impacted? How will my colleagues be impacted? How will my organization be impacted?	
Why do I demonstrate this behavior?	I have developed behaviors over the course of my life because they made sense. What has changed to make this behavior ineffective now?	
How would I like to perform in the future?	Write an end-result statement describing the changes I will make and the impact of those changes. What will an observer see when I have made these changes?	
Who will help me change?	Who could I ask to provide me with feedback on how I am doing? Who could be a good mentor?	
What type of support do I want?	Make an agreement with a person you trust about how you would like to support one another in changing behaviors. How will that person hold me accountable for taking this step? How will I support them in changing their behavior? Is there a group that will support me in the long term?	
What will I do or not do?	What other actions could I take? What am I willing to commit to doing? What am I committed to stopping?	
When will I complete actions?	When will I have completed action items?	

The next template was designed to synthesize development activities reflected in the prior worksheets.

We recommend that all goals be SMART, a term referenced in the November 1981 issue of *Management Review* by George T. Doran. Smart goals comprise five characteristics:

- **Specific** - Goals should be definitive and clearly defined. When goals are specific, it is clear to see when they are reached. To make goals specific, they must clarify exactly what is expected, why it is important, who's involved, where it is going to happen. *Overall example of a goal: Teachers want to improve the reading levels of all the children in our program by 25% in one school year to ensure their future academic success.*

- **Measurable** - Establish concrete criteria for measuring progress toward the attainment of each goal you set. Measurable defines what and how much change we are expecting. *Example: 25% in one school year is the measurement.*

- **Attainable** - When you identify goals that are most important to you, you begin to figure out ways you can make them come true. You develop the attitudes, abilities, skills, and financial capacity to reach them. You begin seeing previously overlooked opportunities to bring yourself closer to the achievement of your goals. "Attainable" ensures that our expectations are reasonable. *Example: One school year and 25% are reasonable goals; 80% in one semester is not an attainable goal.*

- **Realistic** - To be realistic, a goal must represent an objective toward which you are both willing and able to work. A goal can be both high and realistic. You are the only one who can decide the height of your goal, but be sure that every goal represents substantial progress. "Realistic" ensures we have the capacity to meet our goal. *Example: 25% is also realistic. Our children can improve that amount in a year.*

- **Timely** - A goal should be grounded within an approximate time frame. Goals lacking time frames also lack urgency. Being timely ensures we have a deadline to meet our goals. As Dan Heath and Chip Heath state in *Switch: How to Change Things When Change is Hard,* "Some is not a number. Soon is not a time." *Example: One school year is a defined period of time.*

Using the information from the worksheets and templates provided, you are now ready to complete your Development Planning Worksheet. This worksheet will serve as the foundation for the actions you will take to accomplish your goals, and should reflect your data gathering in the assessment chapter and your personal reflection.

TABLE 5-3: DEVELOPMENT PLANNING WORKSHEET
Development Planning Worksheet

Current State	Future State / Goal	Actions	By When?	Measure - How do you know?

Joey's Development Journey Continued

Joey will now walk through her worksheets and journal entries for planning her journey. When we last met Joey she had completed analyzing her situation and strengths.

Joey's Development Plan

DEVELOPMENT PLANNING WORKSHEET – JOEY'S EXAMPLE

Current State	Future State/ Goal	Actions	By When?	Measurement – How do you know?
I would like to hire better so I can fire less often	▪ Educate self on best practices for interviewing ▪ Improve hiring process ▪ Improve on-boarding process	▪ Think through what I want in each open position ▪ Write behavior-based interview questions ▪ Ask value-based questions ▪ Create new staff orientation	Before the next position is posted or within six months	Better teamwork 50% improvement in employee morale 40% improved staff retention
Assessed physical and emotional health through metrics, such as weight, exercise habits, emotional resiliency, etc. I have work to do	Become more emotionally centered and physically healthier	1. Meditation 2. Exercise regularly 3. Mindful eating	Focus on these actions over the next six months	Increased sense of overall well-being and comfort in own skin Re-assess using previous metrics
Improve major donor cultivation process, including overcoming my own reluctance	Grow donor base and unrestricted operating income	1. Create resource development plan 2. Identify prospects and begin cultivating 3. Review previous training on fund raising 4. Ask!	One year	25% increase in unrestricted income Improved skill set

Innovative Leadership Reflection Questions

To help you develop your action plan, it is time to further clarify your direction using reflection questions. The questions for "What do I think/believe?" reflect your intentions. "What do I do?" questions reflect your actions. The questions "What do we believe?" reflect the culture of your organization (i.e., work, school, community), and "How do we do this?" questions reflect systems and processes for your organization. This exercise is an opportunity to practice innovative leadership by considering your vision for yourself and how it will play out in the context of your life. You will define your intentions, actions, culture, and systems in a systematic manner.

Table 5-4 contains an exhaustive list of questions to appeal to a broad range of readers. You will likely find that a few of these best fit your own personal situation. Focus on the questions that seem the most relevant. We recommend you answer one to three questions from each of the categories.

TABLE 5-4: QUESTIONS TO GUIDE THE LEADER AND ORGANIZATION

What do I think/believe?

- What are my priorities for development? Are they reflected in the plan I created?
- Am I willing to make the changes necessary to meet my goals?
- What do I consider personal short-term wins?
- What wins do I want to see in what time frame? Is this reasonable?
- What do I consider a win for my team?
- What do I consider a win for the organization?
- Which short-term wins will be really important to key people in my life?
- How do I stay motivated to work toward goals that will take a long time or a lifetime to accomplish? How will I think about life changes, such as changing eating habits vs. dieting?
- Have I taken into account the whole range of activities I need to create a sustainable change, such as involving others and creating a plan that I can live with long term?

What do I do?

- How do I translate my vision into long and short-term goals?
- Are my goals SMART?
- What are my financial goals and milestones?
- Is this a plan that is sustainable in the long term? Will accomplishing my short-term wins motivate me to stay on track with my long-term plan?
- Does my plan contain the foundation work as well as skill building (example: basic health as well as business competencies)?
- Which wins can I identify and support that solve problems and are seeds for future shifts?
- Which changes in my behavior will demonstrate a strong statement to others and encourage their ongoing support, while possibly modeling changes that could also serve them?

What do we believe?

- Which wins will provide meaningful tangible and emotional results, and gain support of key stakeholders in my life?

- Which wins will encourage others to engage in their own personal/professional growth initiatives?

- Which stories can we tell others about the wins that were shared with the organization to encourage them to focus on their development?

- Which wins are reinforced by our culture and values? Which wins would be opposed to our culture and values?

How do we do this?

- How do I align my goals and short-term wins with the organization such that I receive support for the changes I am making? How do I ensure that early wins are important to key stakeholders?

- How do I track and measure my wins and their impact against overall personal and organizational goals? Do I have early warning measures?

- Are my wins aligned with the larger organizational objectives?

- Does the organization reinforce and reward the behavioral changes I am making?

- How will I connect my personal wins to the organizational vision and measures to demonstrate the impact of my small steps forward?

Joey's Reflection Responses

We will now walk through Joey's answers to one or two questions from each section of Table 5-4. Simply follow along with Joey to answer the questions for yourself or select the questions that fit your current situation.

What do I think/believe?

- *What do I consider personal short-term wins?*

  In the short term, I am focused on trying to understand what is important to as many of our stakeholders as possible (perspective taking). Given the amount of transition we have experienced, coupled with our need for innovative leadership, I am finding that things I took for granted are changing rather rapidly. For that reason, I need to find ways to appear confident so the people who work for me can focus on their jobs rather than worry about what will happen next. I will continue to use meditation and grounding techniques and a solid workout regimen to promote this sense of calm. This is both a short-term and long-term goal. I do not see it as something I will accomplish only once, but, rather, as something I will need to maintain long term. This will require that I change how I look at taking care of myself, as I have tended to just put my head down and work more when the pressure rises, then get burned out. I have always been overly goal-focused, and now I see that the only way I will be able to maintain my balance long term is to take time every day to take care of myself.

- *What do I consider a win for the organization?*

  Nonprofits have to have excellent internal systems and those systems need to be understood and respected by the outside community. A win for the organization at this point will be the increased respect of our community. We have greatly improved our programming and the children we serve are safer, receiving higher-quality programming and being served by better trained staff. The next step is to build our reputation. We need to demonstrate to the community that we've improved and have re-engaged those who had stopped supporting us. When we have succeeded in building the systems, the program, and our reputation there will be no limit to the impact we can make!

What do I do?

- *Are my goals SMART?*

  I used the worksheets provided, and my goals fit the SMART criteria. Because I spent so many years writing grants, it felt very natural to use that model. I know I will continue to refine them as I go, but they are good enough to start. An example is that I will make time every day for self-care—like eating well, spending time with my family, and tending to myself and my needs. I may also do walking meditation so I can get some exercise while I am meditating and reflecting. I know a lot of executives work more than 60 hours per week, but I don't. I'm pretty fast in completing my work. I also know that my organization won't be healthy if I'm not healthy, so I try to live and model that philosophy.

- *How do I translate my vision into long and short-term goals?*

  My vision is to build a successful organization that greatly impacts the youth we are privileged to serve. Short term that means I create buy-in and build the systems to ensure that eventuality. We will create a strategic plan together, which will then be distilled into tactical plans with timelines for each objective and assigned to the right staff or committee to be implemented. Every system will be reviewed including board development, resource development, programming, human resources, facilities, and anything else that comes up. Each opportunity that arises during the process will be measured against the goals and aligned with the vision. How that happens is the longer-term process and is also the path we will follow to implement our values and achieve our vision of being the most successful, best run, and well-respected organization making the largest impact on children in our community.

- *Am I willing to take the actions required to generate these wins?*

  I am willing to take the actions necessary to succeed. I have always been focused on what my work will bring to the world. I am very motivated by the impact I am making on our clients, our community, and my part of the world. While I want to succeed, my definition of success is broad—and is more about the organization than about me personally. I love being the front man for the organization and the center of attention when youth development is the topic; when the center of attention is me, I am far less comfortable.

What do we believe?

◼ *Which stories can we tell others about the wins that were shared with the organization to encourage them to focus on their development?*

Look what we've accomplished! When we meet our goals, we will be able to share our story and inspire others to affect change in their organizations. We took an organization that was three months from closing its doors, with untrained and underperforming staff, and—though it was meeting some of the needs of its families—had very few rules that were inconsistently applied in a program that was not respected in its community. We transformed that organization into one of the most respected agencies in the community with a best practice program, a high-profile board, talented staff, a significant endowment, and well-kept facilities that inspire hope.

How do we do this?

◼ *How will I connect my personal wins to the organizational vision and measurements to demonstrate the impact of my small steps forward?*

As I am the leader of this organization, and people buy into leadership, I am credited with our successes or failures. That makes even the smallest step larger and more intimidating. It's not always fair, or even accurate, as my staff does incredible work and I find ways to credit and honor them for that. Still, I must be courageous to move my organization forward and my professional development is critical as people depend on me—to oversee the safety of their children and/or to ensure their employment. It's a heavy burden, but one I carry with pride. I know what this organization can become, and it is my job to lead us toward that vision.

◼ *Does the organization reinforce and reward the behavioral changes I am making?*

I am fortunate that they do support the changes. Specifically, we are facing significant organizational pressure every day, and my behavior directly impacts the ability of our employees to meet our families' needs. Additionally, I am making tough decisions that change on a daily basis. I need to have a clear head and emotional balance to work under this type of pressure. We are at an important and volatile place and my performance is critical to our success.

Your Process of Creating Your Development Plan

Now that you have followed Joey's descriptions, it is time to complete the worksheets. Based on your assessment results, if you have not done so already, complete the SWOT analysis in Table

4-1 and answer one to three questions from each section in Table 4-2 for yourself. By internalizing your strengths, as well as opportunities, you can identify the gaps that, when filled, will help you accomplish your vision. Additionally, understanding your weaknesses will help you know what to avoid, what to improve, and what personal feedback to request from people skilled in those areas.

This chapter provided you with the tools and templates to create your development plan, and will help to close the gap between where you are today compared with your vision. The plan will greatly enhance your efforts toward actualizing where you want to be, as well as making a positive impact on the world. Keep in mind that it is easy to create a plan that is too ambitious or complex. We encourage you to commit to small changes you can complete and then update your plan after you have accomplished your initial goals. The next chapter focuses on selecting the guiding team that will help you implement your plan.

Additional Resources

Books
Path of Least Resistance: Learning to Become the Creative Force in Your Own Life. Robert Fritz.

Action Inquiry: The Secret of Timely and Transforming Leadership. William R. Torbert.

Crucial Conversations: Tools for Talking when Stakes are High. Kerry Patterson, Joseph Grenny, Ron McMillan, and Al Switzler.

Switch: How to Change Things When Change Is Hard. Chip Heath and Dan Heath.

Fifth Discipline Fieldbook: Strategies and Tools for Building a Learning Organization. Art Kleiner, Peter Senge, Richard Ross, Bryan Smith, Charlotte Roberts.

The Life We Were Given: A Long Term Program for Realizing Potential of Body, Mind, Heart and Soul. George Leonard and Michael Murphy.

Polarity Management: Identifying and Managing Unsolvable Problems. Barry Johnson.

DVDs
Integral Life Practice Starter Kit. Integral Institute (3-2-1 shadow workshop and Big Mind).

All Quadrants All Levels Framework (AQAL). Ken Wilber.

CD
Mindfulness in Motion – A Daily Low Dose Mindfulness Practice. Maryanna Klatt, Ph.D.

Online resource and tools
HeartMath™ meditation practices and emWave to monitor heart activity. www.heartmath.org

Integral Transformative Practice. www.itp-international.org

What do I think/believe?

What do I do?

_____

_____

_____

_____

_____

_____

_____

_____

_____

_____

_____

_____

_____

_____

_____

_____

_____

_____

_____

_____

_____

_____

_____

What do we believe?

How do we do this?

TABLE 5-2: SKILL/BEHAVIOR DEVELOPMENT WORKSHEET
Evaluate and Select Skill/Behavioral Change Priorities – Worksheet

Key Actions	Detailed Action Planning	Behavior 2
Select behaviors	Which behaviors do I want to improve or change? Which behaviors do I perform well that I would like to enhance?	
What are the consequences of this behavior?	What will happen if I continue to demonstrate this behavior in the future? How will my service recipients be impacted? How will my career be impacted? How will my colleagues be impacted? How will my organization be impacted?	
Why do I demonstrate this behavior?	I have developed behaviors over the course of my life because they made sense. What has changed to make this behavior ineffective now?	
How would I like to perform in the future?	Write an end-result statement describing the changes I will make and the impact of those changes. What will an observer see when I have made these changes?	
Who will help me change?	Who could I ask to provide me with feedback on how I am doing? Who could be a good mentor?	
What type of support do I want?	Make an agreement with a person you trust about how you would like to support one another in changing behaviors. How will that person hold me accountable for taking this step? How will I support them in changing their behavior? Is there a group that will support me in the long term?	
What will I do or not do?	What other actions could I take? What am I willing to commit to doing? What am I committed to stopping?	
When will I complete actions?	When will I have completed action items?	

TABLE 5-2: SKILL/BEHAVIOR DEVELOPMENT WORKSHEET
Evaluate and Select Skill/Behavioral Change Priorities – Worksheet

Key Actions	Detailed Action Planning	Behavior 3
Select behaviors	Which behaviors do I want to improve or change? Which behaviors do I perform well that I would like to enhance?	
What are the consequences of this behavior?	What will happen if I continue to demonstrate this behavior in the future? How will my service recipients be impacted? How will my career be impacted? How will my colleagues be impacted? How will my organization be impacted?	
Why do I demonstrate this behavior?	I have developed behaviors over the course of my life because they made sense. What has changed to make this behavior ineffective now?	
How would I like to perform in the future?	Write an end-result statement describing the changes I will make and the impact of those changes. What will an observer see when I have made these changes?	
Who will help me change?	Who could I ask to provide me with feedback on how I am doing? Who could be a good mentor?	
What type of support do I want?	Make an agreement with a person you trust about how you would like to support one another in changing behaviors. How will that person hold me accountable for taking this step? How will I support them in changing their behavior? Is there a group that will support me in the long term?	
What will I do or not do?	What other actions could I take? What am I willing to commit to doing? What am I committed to stopping?	
When will I complete actions?	When will I have completed action items?	

CHAPTER 6

Step 4: Build Your Team & Communicate

In this chapter, you will begin to identify the individuals you want to support your personal and professional development, and the specific roles you envision them playing during this transition. After selecting these people, you will consider the best ways to communicate your needs and receive their feedback. Here, you will carefully choose individuals you feel will be most supportive of your growth. Consider who is involved in your development and who is not. Your selection criteria should include: experience and skills in areas you want to develop, level of unconditional personal support, ability to offer constructive and valuable feedback, capacity to support your transformation, and ability to offer professional support and advocacy.

You will benefit from choosing a diverse yet trusted set of people to support your development. This is particularly beneficial if you plan to make changes that will significantly impact them as well. These people can come from various areas of your life, both personal and professional, and can have differing levels of involvement. Some, for example, could be fairly casual, such as a co-worker who is willing to give you feedback after a meeting about a specific behavior you may be experimenting with to meet a goal about improved interpersonal skills. At the other end of the spectrum, you could engage in a more methodical, long-term agreement with a formal mentor or coach. You will also want to consider the role your spouse or partner plays if you are involved in a relationship. Anyone involved must agree to give you honest and supportive feedback. The common thread for the people you ultimately invite to share in your journey is a firm trust and belief that, above all else, their support is unquestionably in the interest and service of your growth and success.

As another option, your development support could be found within a team setting. For example, if your goal is to run a marathon, your development support could come from a range of sources. It could be as simple as joining a running group to support a fitness goal. You might recruit very specific individual running partners. Other options could include finding expertise from third-party sources like running magazines or online groups that discuss tips and progress. You may even select a group where the explicit purpose is to strongly hold each other more accountable.

Professional development can be supported in similar ways. You have a broad range of choices when looking for support. Organizations range from coaching and training firms to companies that help you improve your presentation skills. Depending on your needs, your individual selection of development support may have components of some or all of these choices. Some may be focused on hard skills, while others, like a coach, take on a more generally supportive role.

After you have selected your support team, the next step will be deciding on methods for each person to communicate authentic feedback. This is the stage where you ask others for specific kinds of support, including possible behavioral changes on their part. You will be letting people around you know that you are engaged in a process of ambitious personal growth and that you want their feedback. Because people often create a sense of personal safety by being able to predict how others around them behave, it is important to inform the people closest to you that you are taking on a structured change process that may involve behaviors with which they are likely to be unfamiliar. The key message here should convey that this process will take time and you will use these new behaviors with varying levels of effectiveness until you master them. You may say you are changing and yet act inconsistently for some period of time while you master new skills.

While the information you share will change over time, the need for communication is critical throughout your development process. Communication will happen with different groups of people at various times, and will likely take on different tones depending on the audience and degree of impact. Some people will simply need to understand that overall change is underway. You will want others to make significant contributions to support your behavioral change. What you communicate and when will depend on your relationship with the individual or group, and the type of support you are asking for.

During your process, you may also be asking others to change. For example, in the workplace, you may be communicating information beyond just the scope of work in order to help your staff, coworkers, associates, employees, and direct reports develop stronger business acumen. Moreover, you may want others to change their overall style of communication with you. As you model these new behaviors, be aware that some of your colleagues will adapt quite naturally, while others will require more specific and formal discussions to adjust to this new way of relating. As another example, you may want to delegate more and possibly different tasks, as well as give people more freedom to determine how they accomplish assigned tasks. In this case, you could open a dialogue explaining that you are trusting them to determine the most effective approach and will be available to offer support if additional input is needed. Though many employees would respond favorably to the openness, some will likely be confused if you are not explicit with what you are trying to accomplish.

Support Team Selection Criteria

Providing support to someone who is committed to a process of personal growth is an honor and a tremendous responsibility. It is important to select a support team judiciously since you are asking these individuals to be trusted advisors.

The following is a rough list of key selection factors as a starting point for you to consider when selecting your team. You may find other factors that are also important to you.

Performance: Consider selecting people who have mastered concepts, skills, or behaviors that you would like to develop in yourself. Performance could be as simple as that person having expertise in your field, or a field you want to explore. He could have strong interpersonal skills and empathy, or have hard skills such as financial analysis that you would like to enhance in yourself. These individuals could also be people you respect in general. If you are focused on developing advanced leadership skills, you could certainly benefit from the mentoring and support of someone you believe is successful against these measures.

Coaching: Consider having a person who is paid as an independent expert in the process of development or therapy. Most have undergone rigorous training or have significant experience in the field to support your development and success. As they are independent, they are generally free of the natural bias held by family members, friends, and colleagues. Working with the right coach can be very valuable, significantly accelerate the development process, and help you overcome barriers.

Therapy: Having someone who is an experienced psychotherapist can be very beneficial. A good therapist who is a good fit with your style and needs can help you make changes much more quickly and efficiently than if you try to work through issues yourself.

Personal or Family Connection: People from your family supporting your development could include siblings, a partner or a spouse, or a close friend who feels like family. Ideally, they will help you maintain a balanced perspective of your life as a whole based on a historical connection, rather than just the immediate view of a new coach or therapist. They will also help you think through the impact of your changes on your family system. It is important to balance your development and professional focus with your family commitments.

Willingness and ability to commit time to your development: This is imperative. Ask those committed to supporting your development how to optimize your time together, and also discuss your mutual needs. The idea is that everyone should benefit from a clear understanding of how to both support the growth process and create healthy reciprocity. It will also be important to consider the time commitment you desire. Be willing to explore options that allow you to minimize the amount of time you request. You may consider creative options like volunteering for a board that your mentor or support person is on. This would allow you to learn directly and also support that person in meeting their objectives.

Consider not only who to select but also who to avoid. Keep in mind that there are many very well-meaning people who would love to help, but, realistically, who are overcommitted and cannot provide the type of support you seek. Others may lack strong support skills, like the ability to give open and honest feedback. If someone lacks the time or skills to provide helpful advice, delivered in a supportive way, you should not include them. What you do not need during an intense development process is to waste time and energy with someone whose involvement could derail you.

Tools

The following worksheets are designed to help you connect your development action plan with the people who will help you accomplish these goals. They will fulfill different roles, ranging from encouragement and support to providing skilled expertise. You might also choose to include those who may be more directly impacted by the changes you are making. The more information you can provide during the process, the more likely they will be to support you or communicate their concerns to help you accomplish your goals. For an example, see Joey's answers following each worksheet.

TABLE 6-1: SUPPORT TEAM WORKSHEET				
Support Team Worksheet				
Goal	Type of Support I Need	Role	Skills/ Knowledge or Other Criteria	Arrangement

Joey's Development Journey Continued

When we last connected with Joey, she had created her development plan. She is now evaluating who will help her implement her goals.

SUPPORT TEAM WORKSHEET – JOEY'S SAMPLE

Goal	Type of Support I Need	Role	Skills/ Knowledge	Arrangement
Increase effectiveness: ▬ Become more adept at seeing multiple perspectives and comfortable with allowing results to emerge rather than controlling them	Coach	▬ Gives me exercises and practices ▬ Provides feedback on behavioral experiments ▬ Open to practicing new behaviors	Multiple-level perspective taking and comfort with ambiguity	Paid - Weekly conversations
Become more emotionally centered and physically healthier	Healthy colleagues, board, and staff	▬ Reinforce healthy behaviors ▬ Provide feedback on behavioral experiments ▬ Open to practicing new behaviors	Healthy practices	Mentoring/Mutual support
	Healthy friends	▬ Engage in and reinforce healthy behaviors ▬ Provide feedback on behavioral experiments ▬ Open to practicing new behaviors	Healthy practices	Mutual support
Grow the organization	Colleagues/ mentor	▬ Another executive ▬ Talk through options	Program, reputation, resource development, and board growth	Collegial

Once you determine your support team and their corresponding roles, you will want to figure out communication, timing, and expectations. This is the place to consider the kind of feedback you might expect from others to ensure you are making meaningful progress. This communication can provide you with invaluable information and feedback that is critical for your success. Since your plan is based on your own intuitive senses, the ongoing data should confirm your assumptions and serve as a feedback mechanism to refine your thinking.

TABLE 6-2: COMMUNICATION PLAN WORKSHEET
Communication Planning Worksheet

Who	What to Communicate	What They Can Expect From You	What You Want From Them	How Often

The following table is from Joey's Communication Worksheet. You can use it as an example of how one may use communication when managing change both personally and within an organization.

COMMUNICATION PLANNING WORKSHEET – JOEY'S SAMPLE

Who	What to Communicate	What They Can Expect From You	What You Want From Them	How Often
Husband	How am I doing against my major goals? How are my changes impacting you? Us? Practice inquiry skills	As I become more centered, my reactions to difficult issues will be more thoughtful As I learn to take more perspectives, I will offer additional insights and also ask questions to better understand his perspective Additional questions about how my "behavioral experiments" are doing	Listening Feedback Recommendations	Check in daily
Leadership Team	How am I doing against my major goals? How are my changes impacting you? Us? Practice inquiry skills Share reflections and ask for their reflections	As I become more centered, my reactions to difficult issues will be more thoughtful As I learn to take more perspectives, I will offer additional insights and also ask questions to better understand their perspectives Grow the organization in ways we jointly define and refine Additional questions about how my "behavioral experiments" are doing Discussions that contain additional reflections to provide more context for decision making	Listening Feedback Recommendations	Check in 2x per month
Friends	I am making some personal changes and I would like feedback as I try new behaviors	Additional questions about how my "behavioral experiments" are doing Discussions that contain additional reflections to provide more contexts for decision making	Feedback Recommendations	Ad hoc

Innovative Leadership Reflection Questions

To help you develop your action plan, it is time to further clarify your direction using reflection questions. The questions for "What do I think/believe?" reflect your intentions. "What do I do?" questions reflect your actions. The questions "What do we believe?" reflect the culture of your organization (i.e., work, school, community), and "How do we do this?" questions reflect systems and processes for your organization. This exercise is an opportunity to practice innovative leadership by considering your vision for yourself and how it will play out in the context of your life. You will define your intentions, actions, culture, and systems in a systematic manner.

Table 6-3 contains an exhaustive list of questions to appeal to a broad range of readers. A few will likely fit your own personal situation; focus on the ones that seem the most relevant. We recommend you answer one to three questions from each of the categories.

TABLE 6-3: QUESTIONS TO GUIDE THE LEADER AND ORGANIZATION

What do I think/believe?

- What qualities do I want in the people I ask to support my personal change?
- What qualities will I eliminate from my current and future team?
- How do I think my change will impact those close to me?
- Will my change help those close to me become more successful according to their definition of success?
- Why would others spend their time and energy to help me develop?
- How much support do I expect from others?
- Am I making reasonable requests of those close to me?
- Am I looking for others in the social service arena who are making similar changes?
- Do I want people around me to change along with me?
- Do I need to improve my communication skills to improve my ability to seek support for my growth? Do I understand that my effectiveness at communicating to others, as well as listening to their feedback, hinges on my ability to communicate effectively?
- Because my development may be a very personal and even private choice, what am I willing to communicate to others?
- How do I think my preference for privacy or sharing will impact others' responses to my changes and their ability to do what they need to do to either support me or accomplish their jobs? Do I solicit their input and support? If so, how and when?
- What personal stories (actions and emotions) will convey my commitment to my personal change in a heartfelt manner while also empowering others to act?
- Do I need to communicate anything to the organization or just to my support group?

What do I do?

- Who do I ask to participate in my change?
- How do I determine and communicate the criteria for the right people to support me? "Right" includes personality traits, innate capabilities, skills, knowledge, time, and willingness

- Once I know the criteria, who are the right people and how do I figure out what roles I would like them to take to support my success? How do I invite them to support this important personal transformation?

- Who do I need to support my development for it to be successful? How can my personal development activities or successes help these key people meet their personal objectives?

- Who may become a barrier to my change? How do I mitigate their negative impact? What are immediate steps and longer-term actions?

- What commitments and actions should I take that demonstrate my belief that change is possible?

- How do I "walk the talk" and show my conviction through my actions? Am I making the changes I say I will? Am I asking for input and acting on the recommendations others give me? If I do not take their recommendations, do I explain why?

- How do I ask for feedback? Am I clear about what information would be helpful to me and what information would not be helpful?

- How do I convey my request for input and support when I fall short of my stated goals at points along the way?

- How do I deliver messages tailored to different supporters that motivate them to continue to help me accomplish my goals?

- Can I be a role model for others during my change process to encourage them to expand their own capabilities?

- How do I convey messages that will make strong statements using the languages of both feelings and logic to appeal to each individual supporter?

- How do I demonstrate humility and genuinely appreciate the support others are providing?

- How do I communicate progress, new challenges, and my commitment to what I am doing?

- How do I communicate the facts and my hopes for the future?

- How do I communicate that the balance between challenge and overload is important, and that I want to maintain balance as I move toward meeting my personal vision?

- How do I communicate my need and desire for accurate feedback?

- What do I communicate when my situation and priorities change?

What do we believe?

- What are the social and cultural norms that dictate the type of support I should ask for and expect?

- How do we use my personal change as an opportunity to test new behaviors and demonstrate their positive impact on the group (professional organization, family, community)?

- Do the current social and cultural norms still fit for where I am/we are going?

- Do I have the right support to change the culture of our group to allow me to sustain the changes I am trying to make?

- What are our beliefs about who does the communicating? How much information do they share? How often? Do we solicit input or just convey information?

- What is the appropriate language and message content based on the values, goals, language, and culture of each audience segment (organization, family, community)?

- What type of feedback will I seek from supporters to determine if they are supportive of my personal changes? This may be objective or subjective

- Does our current organizational culture and approach to communicating support me in making the changes I am trying to make?

How do we do this?

- What are the key skills and behaviors that support my transformation and are necessary to my team? What are the gaps between my current support team and the team needed to support transformation? Do I have the right people available with the right skills and behaviors? Do I need to augment my support team with professionals such as a coach, therapist, spiritual advisor, clergy, colleague, or boss?

- What is the best combination of approaches for me to meet my support needs? Does this include hiring a coach or scheduling regular lunches with a trusted colleague?

- What trust-building activities can we conduct to improve my degree of comfort with those supporting me?

- What personal and professional metrics should I track to understand if I am seeking and receiving the appropriate level of support?

- If the transformation is a long one, how do I acknowledge the support others are providing? What happens if someone I thought would be a good supporter does not work out, such as a colleague changing jobs or moving out of the area?

- Am I communicating what supporters believe is important to them? Do they see the progress they hope to see?

- How do I communicate wins to stakeholders to sustain their reinforcement and energy?

- What is my communication approach and plan? Who wants information? When? Through what medium? What are the key messages? How do I keep multiple supporters informed with the right amount of information at the right time to enhance buy-in and support for my behavioral change?

- Do we have any applicable stories connected with group folklore? ("Remember the time xxx did xxx? Guess what happened to me this week.")

- Can we combine and/or eliminate any current communications? Are we talking about things that are not supportive of the change I want to make?

- Would communication be more effective if my changes were discussed in conjunction with other topics that either impact or are impacted by my change? If as a group we are trying to change, maybe we can talk about our progress, or about personal and organizational changes and how they are linked and impact one another

Joey's Response to Reflection Questions

We will now walk through Joey's answers to one or two questions from each section of Table 6-3. Simply follow along with Joey to answer the questions for yourself, or select the questions that fit your current situation.

What do I think/believe?

- *What qualities do I want in the people I ask to support my personal change?*

  I want my team to give me candid feedback, yet also be gentle. I expect this work to be difficult for me, and while I am committed to improving as a leader, I want to my team to be kind in their suggestions.

- *Am I looking for others in the social service arena who are making similar changes?*

  I am not. I am looking for leaders who can help me be transformational; I do not think they need to have gone through a similar process. If they have, it may be helpful, but it is not critical to the formation of my team. I want them to demonstrate the skills I seek.

■ *How do I think my change will impact those close to me?*

I hope it will allow me to be a better leader eventually. The changes I am making may feel disconcerting or even disingenuous to my management team because even though they may not have liked the old behaviors they understood how to work with or around them.

■ *Because my personal development is a very personal and even private choice, what am I willing to communicate to others?*

I believe that my growth and development is a private matter, so I only discuss it in depth with people I trust. While I want to model a focus on development, most people do not need to know the details of my goals and plans. Because I am the CEO, it is important to balance what I share and what remains personal. I want to be transparent, yet also maintain the respect from my staff and board.

As I become more comfortable in my current space, I'm more open about sharing my vision with people and finding great support. It is both the vision itself and my passion that I think people are responding to in a very positive manner. I am surprised and delighted to see this reaction. I am not sure why I would think otherwise, but that is the case.

What do I do?

■ *Who do I want to ask to participate in my change?*

I have asked my husband to be a primary development partner because he knows me better than anyone else. He will also be the most affected by many of the changes I make. I have also asked a board member I respect, one of my direct reports whom I trust, and a few colleagues. I am looking for different information from each. I will walk through many things with my husband, and seek feedback from my colleagues, the board and staff member who see me in different roles and who can provide different observations.

■ *How do I convey my request for input and support when I fall short of my stated goals at points along the way?*

This can be difficult. I am easily embarrassed when I do not meet my own standards or the commitments I have made to others. I have found that this group's expectations are not as high as my personal ones. I am grateful in some ways and disappointed in others. Since I have such high personal standards, I often beat myself up over an incident; I've discovered that I need to be kinder to myself. My husband is wonderful in helping me realize that and always reminds me that even when I think I could have done something better, others involved are often satisfied with the results or how I handled that particular situation. As I previously started, his feedback is not particularly objective, but it is wonderful to have his unconditional support!

What do we believe?

■ *Do I have the right support to change the culture of our group to allow me to sustain the changes I am trying to make?*

I'm not sure. I hope so, but don't know yet. It is always a bit scary to invite a board member to whom you report and an employee who reports to you to help with your own professional development. I think and hope it will be worth the vulnerable position in which I have put myself.

■ *What are our beliefs about communication with regard to who does the communicating? How much information do they share? How often? Do we solicit input or just convey information?*

Soliciting input is quite important for me to know how I am being received and how I can improve. I continue to seek a great deal of feedback to understand how much information people want from me, how often, and in what format. I meet with each of my direct reports weekly and end each meeting with a check in of how we are doing. From the input I get, I created a structured communication plan to help me track what people want to ensure I am meeting their expectations.

How do we do this?

■ *What is the best combination of approaches for me to meet my support needs? Does this include hiring a coach or scheduling regular lunches with a trusted colleague?*

I have built the team of my husband, a board member, and a staff member, and am receiving incredible support and feedback in my effort to reach my goals. I also invited a few trusted colleagues into the mix. Yet, other than my husband, I found that I was not being completely honest about my fears—because of that I also hired a coach. As one of my team supervises me and the other is supervised by me, the power dynamics got in the way in certain cases. Even in the case of my colleagues, I found myself worrying about what they thought of me. My new coach has helped me to be completely honest about my hopes, dreams, weaknesses, and goals, and because of that, I am moving forward faster.

■ *What is my communication approach and plan? Who wants feedback? When? Through what medium? From who? What are the key messages? How do I keep multiple supporters informed with the right amount of information at the right time to enhance buy-in and influence my behavioral change?*

During my transition, I am defining new communication approaches. I am asking all of these questions of myself and my management team to ensure that I am communicating the information they are seeking. I am also taking care to keep my support team abreast of my successes and failures. Because I tend to mull over the failures and focus on what I could have done differently, my tendency is to gloss over the successes. I am trying to introduce a culture of celebrating small victories.

Your Individual Process to Build Your Team and Communicate

Now that you have seen the worksheets and read through Joey's narratives, it is time to complete the worksheets and answer the questions for yourself if you have not done so already. We encourage you to complete all of the exercises. Based on your support preferences, complete Table 6-1 (Support Team worksheet) and Table 6-2 (Communication Planning worksheet), then answer one to three questions from each section in Table 6-3.

This chapter serves to help you clarify your supporters and communication plan as you begin defining your feedback sources. This is the plan that will provide you with expertise, emotional support, buy-in, and feedback for your development. While creating a communication plan may seem extraneous, never underestimate the value of both emotional, moral support, and communication with those who will be affected by your changes. This could be as simple as talking to your spouse or family about the way your changing routine may impact them, while letting them know you appreciate their willingness to be flexible.

Resources

Book:
Crucial Conversations: Tools for Talking when Stakes are High. Patterson, Grenny, McMillan, Switzler.

Fifth Discipline Fieldbook: Strategies and Tools for Building a Learning Organization. Kleiner, Senge, Ross, Smith, Roberts.

What do I think/believe?

What do I do?

What do we believe?

How do we do this?

CHAPTER 7
Step 5: Take Action

Now that you have created a plan to become an innovative leader and have defined your support team, it is time to take action. Your plan should spell out which actions you want to take, how often, and who can support your progress.

As you begin realizing your vision, you may start to identify challenges to your growth and development. Barriers are simply a normal part of any transformative process; we have provided a number of useful tools to help pinpoint and navigate them successfully.

An important part of your success is believing that you can make progress and sustain growth in your leadership ability. You developed a strong foundation by creating a compelling vision and analyzed unique challenges and opportunities to determine what actions you needed to take to achieve your goals.

Be aware that this stage can take tremendous focus and energy. Many people stumble here, especially when the change process becomes difficult and the demands of balancing life requirements take on greater urgency. Think, for example, of how many times you may have joined a gym, but did not follow your plan to go there as frequently as you'd intended. Implementing your plan requires a deep commitment to your growth and also an understanding of the barriers you will face based on your personality type or history with implementing change. As barriers surface, you have the ability to remove them or modify your course with the support of your team.

With this in mind, allow yourself some flexibility in your development process instead of viewing your plan as fixed. See your plan as an initial starting point, or a working hypothesis about how you will develop. With that perspective, you can better use the challenges you face as a way to provide feedback on your original hypothesis and modify it as you go along. In other words, rather than viewing these obstacles as threats, you have the opportunity to naturally incorporate them as fine-tuning mechanisms. For each challenge you face, carefully consider the unique learning opportunity and how to use it to help you implement your plan. Since personal development is a long-term journey, you will have many opportunities to face these challenges and take corrective actions.

Lastly, your support team will play a crucial role in helping make the plan sustainable. They will offer you input and feedback as well as encouragement during times when you struggle. Even though you specifically chose the changes and goals within your plan, it is often still helpful to have a built-in system of accountability. When you run into inner resistance and difficulty, connect with someone who will remind you that you are already competent and that you can meet these goals in the same way you have met many other challenges.

Tools

The following worksheet helps you to anticipate barriers and mitigate them while implementing your action plan. You can refer to Joey's completed worksheets as an example.

TABLE 7-1: BARRIERS ACTION PLANNING WORKSHEET				
Category	Barrier	Impact of Barrier	How to Remove or Work Around	Support I Need to Remove or Work Around
In my thinking				
In my behavior				
In our beliefs				
In how we do things				

Joey's Development Journey Continued

When we last met Joey, she was building her support team and defining how she wanted to communicate.

BARRIER ACTION PLANNING WORKSHEET – JOEY'S SAMPLE

Category	Barrier	Impact of Barrier	How to Remove or Work Around	Support I Need to Remove or Work Around
In my thinking	I think people will continue to expect me to act like I did prior to undertaking this commitment to change and may think I will never really meet my goals	I give up too soon	Go to a friend to remind me "I can" when I feel external pressure and want to give up	Continue to talk to friend weekly to reinforce that I can meet these goals
In my behavior	I assume conflict when it isn't there, or isn't at the level I presume	I miss the opportunity to allow things to unfold	Remind myself to trust the management team	Ask the member of my support team who is on the management team to give me a code word in meetings so I know I am not meeting my goals
In our beliefs	We believe that since we hire smart people they will not need much input or supervision	People do not get the information they need to accomplish their tasks efficiently and with minimal frustration	Slow down and verify that team members and employees have the same understanding about the task outcome and general approach to success, including key milestones, success measures, and deadlines	Partners and team members to demonstrate similar behavior and reinforce it in others by asking if we have done this on key projects
In how we do things	People will continue to expect me to react like I used to, so they will continue to act like they used to	Those expectations will point me in the direction opposite than where I aspire to go	I need to remember and remind myself of my ultimate goal	Share with others my goals, as appropriate, and try to catch myself and them when we start to slip into old roles/habits

Innovative Leadership Reflection Questions

To help you develop your action plan, it is time to further clarify your direction using reflection questions. The questions for "What do I think/believe?" reflect your intentions. "What do I do?" questions reflect your actions. The questions "What do we believe?" reflect the culture of your organization (i.e., work, school, community), and "How do we do this?" questions reflect systems and processes for your organization. This exercise is an opportunity to practice innovative leadership by considering your vision for yourself and how it will play out in the context of your life. You will define your intentions, actions, culture, and systems in a systematic manner.

Table 7-2 contains a thorough list of questions to appeal to a broad range of readers. You will likely find some that best fit your own personal situation; focus on those that seem the most relevant. We recommend you answer one to three questions from each of the categories.

TABLE 7-2: QUESTIONS TO GUIDE THE LEADER AND ORGANIZATION

What do I think/believe?

- In what ways do I need to change my perspective or skills to succeed?
- To become more effective, what do I need to change about how I see myself or the world?
- Including beliefs, what do I need to let go of to make these changes?
- What do I see as my individual role? How does this role allow me to fit in different organizations, including my family?
- How can I effectively grow and empower myself? How do I support my success as well as the success of the organization(s)?
- How can I benefit from my own personal growth and development?

What do I do?

- What feedback do I seek that will allow me to correct, redirect, or recalibrate my behavior and feel motivated to make necessary changes?
- How do I request clear and concise feedback that allows me to grow and supports the growth of others?
- How do I determine what I am ready to change within myself and what additional support I require for those changes I am resisting?
- What help am I willing to request? Am I investing appropriate time and/or money to support my growth? Is the commitment I am making to my personal change consistent with the results I expect to receive?
- What creative solutions can I find to increase my personal awareness? Do I track my performance against my goals using logs or reflection activities?
- How will I identify times when my own behavior undermines my success?
- What will I do when I find my own behavior undermines my success?
- Can I treat my own competing commitments as learning opportunities?
- How do I encourage "bad news" as well as good from my support team?
- Am I looking for opportunities to visibly demonstrate my progress as my development process unfolds?
- What am I doing to retain my support team as time goes on?
- How do I manage my transformation over the passage of time? How do I focus on living my current life while concurrently focusing sufficient time on my vision and goals?

What do we believe?

- How will my changes impact my ability to be successful, based on the organization's reward system, and given its values, goals, and culture?

- What are the stories within the organization about effective leadership? How do my personal changes position me going forward?

- What stories of the past do we need to stop telling because they no longer support our or my success?

- How can we connect prior leadership development successes to my current development effort? How can we use prior success to reinforce our ability to navigate current leadership changes?

- What parts of our past failures were attributed to leadership? Do my development changes appear positive to the organization's success or are they threatening?

- Does our culture support the behavioral traits I am trying to develop?

How do we do this?

- What processes do we have that may serve as barriers to my developing in the way I would like? Am I in a position to change the systems to remove these barriers? If so, how involved and complex will those changes be? If I cannot remove the barriers, how will I navigate around them?

- Are my changes aligned with the organization's guiding principles? If not, how do I navigate the gaps between them?

- Do the organizational structure and governance approach support my personal development? If not, what options do I have to resolve barriers to my growth?

- What early warning metrics can I use to track the impact my behavioral changes are having on others? What leading indicators will alert me before any significant issues arise?

- How can I leverage current or generally accepted mastery frameworks to gain support of others and explain the changes I am trying to make?

- How do my changes fit into the current organizational reward system? If there are misalignments, what will I do to navigate the barriers and challenges?

- Have I clearly articulated the changes I want to make and asked for the support of those around me while allowing them to maintain their success in a dynamic and changing environment?

- What communication processes do we use to provide timely feedback? How will these impact me during my development? How will my development impact others?

- What communication, if any, do I use for those who are not supporting my development?

- What is the organization doing to measure, communicate, and fund the activities required for my development?

Joey's Response to Reflection Questions

We will now walk through Joey's answers to one or two questions from each section of Table 7-2. Simply follow along with Joey to answer the questions for yourself or select the questions that fit your current situation.

What do I think/believe?

- *In what ways do I need to change my perspective or skills to succeed?*

  One of my development goals is to create buy-in with the direct service staff. To do that, I will need to continue to participate in exercises that require me to take multiple perspectives, like the shadow exercise where I look at situations from the perspective of others involved. Perspective-taking is a skill I am working to develop as part of my goals. I will know if I have done this well when I track my progress based on input from others. While this is important work, it is also hard to continue to seek out my own shortcomings. I will do this at a pace I can manage. Accomplishing this goal may help me build the foundation to be more effective.

- *Including beliefs, what do I need to let go of to make these changes?*

  I need to let go of the idea that my way is the only way. On an intellectual level I know and believe that there are multiple ways to accomplish any goal. When under stress, I tend to refer back to the idea that there in only one way. I need to remember that there are many paths to the finish line—the more people who are engaged in the process, the better our team and the stronger our organization.

What do I do?

- *How do I determine what I am ready to change within myself and what additional support I require for those changes I am resisting?*

  I am fascinated by the idea that people occasionally work in direct conflict with their goals. I have to assume that I do that as well, and, in fact if pressed, can think of times when my efforts have been compromised because of roadblocks I introduced. I am hopeful that my team, and especially my coach, can help me to align my actions with my goals.

- *How do I encourage "bad news" as well as good from my support team?*

  I ask for the bad news. I'm pretty direct and have always encouraged feedback, thanked people for sharing it, and reminded them that I cannot grow as a professional without it. I know that negative feedback is hard to give—it's hard for me too—but it's the only way that any of us is going to transcend our current status and become the leaders we aspire to be.

What do we believe?

- *How will my changes impact my ability to be successful based on the organization's reward system, given its values, goals, and culture?*

  I am fortunate to be the CEO of the organization, so my changes should not impact my ability to keep my job. Then again, CEOs serve at the pleasure of the board—so if I move too fast or alienate people in the process, it could become an issue. Always an essential factor, while I am undergoing this process, it is even more critical that I engage all board members in my vision for the organization.

The changes I am making will have an impact on the people with whom I work. As I do things differently, they will be required to do things differently that will impact our culture as well. The changes will be refined as we clarify our organizational goals and services in response to the needs of our community and our goals of being a leading service provider in that community.

- *What stories of the past do we need to stop telling because they no longer support our or my success?*

We need to stop telling the details of the story of our leadership change. Dwelling on the details does nothing more than look backward and remind people of our missteps. The more beneficial story is that the board saw the need for change and put systems in place to ensure that change was made. We want people to focus on where we are going—not where we have been—and engage them toward our future success.

How do we do this?

- *Do the organizational structure and the governance approach support my personal development? If not, what options do I have to remove barriers to my growth?*

One of the interesting concepts we are testing is dynamic steering. We make small decisions and corrective actions that we treat as experiments. Dynamic steering is an element of a larger governance system called Holacracy (www.holacracy.org), and is similar to the process of steering a bicycle—we have a strategic plan and know where we are going, and the ride can be much smoother if we make small, continual corrections rather than sharp, gross corrections. It means we need to be willing to question and change our decisions regularly. That means people will need to be comfortable questioning and being questioned. The questioning phase is where things tend to break down, but it's also the phase where most of the learning occurs.

We aspire to treat most decisions as learning opportunities. This means we develop a hypothesis or idea of what will work and test it. In each test we will learn and refine our thinking. By taking this approach of an action and reflection cycle, we are able to continually learn. This process is well aligned with my personal approach to my development, and also allows me the freedom to try my own new behaviors as experiments. I can experiment with different roles or approaches and learn from these experiments. The model requires people, including me, to become comfortable with change. I am concerned that we will get bogged down by those resisting change. We have a plan to deal with that and have tried to create buy-in and communicate what's coming in an effort to minimize the fear associated with change.

Everyone in the organization has the same opportunity and freedom to try new approaches and offer recommendations. Of course, not everyone has embraced the idea so we are creating redo loops to assure everyone that learning is not about blame and expanding our training to infuse this idea throughout the organization.

Your Process of Taking Action

Now that you have seen the worksheets and read through Joey's narratives, it is time to complete the worksheets and answer the questions. We encourage you to complete all of the exercises and answer one to three reflection questions from each section in Table 7-2. This process serves to help you clarify what your barriers to success are, and how you will manage or remove them.

This chapter summarizes the basics for identifying barriers to your ability to successfully accomplish your goals as described in your plan. It also asks you to monitor the systems you put into place to measure your success and take corrective action. The next chapter will walk you through the process of ensuring that the changes you make are sustainable.

Additional Resources

Book
Action Inquiry: The Secret of Timely and Transforming Leadership. William R. Torbert and Associates.

How the Way We Talk can Change the Way We Work: Seven Languages for Transformation. Robert Kegan and Lisa Laskow Lahey.

DVD
Shadow Module 3-2-1 Process with Diane Hamilton. Integral Life Practice Series produced by Integral Institute.

What do I think/believe?

What do I do?

What do we believe?

How do we do this?

CHAPTER 8
Step 6: Embed Innovation Systematically

Congratulations! You have made it to the final chapter in your development process. You are now ready to shift from implementing your plan as something with a discrete end to considering how you will integrate these changes into your lifestyle going forward. We suggest you view your leadership development as an ongoing process rather than something to check off the to-do list. Given the volume of change we are facing now and expect to face in the future, continual development is a must simply to stay current. In this light, you can begin asking yourself, "What supports can I put into place to stay on track? How can I gain additional benefits from ongoing practice?"

To maintain momentum, it is critical to retain a sense of urgency and minimize any complacency that may come from early success. Be aware that it is easy to stray from your goals if you declare success based on your early results, especially when other areas of your life tug at your time and attention. One helpful shift in thinking is to see the actions you are taking as a practice. You are practicing your leadership skills in the same fashion that a professional athlete practices a particular sport. The most successful athletes are constantly working to improve, even though they may already be the best in the world. This is why many of them remain successful over a long period of time. You will need to consider a long-term commitment to activities that foster success and help maintain your momentum.

So, ask yourself, "When I see progress, what will keep me motivated to continue practicing? I need some reminder that my progress is a result of engaged practice, and my performance is likely to suffer if I do not maintain proper focus."

By this point, you may want to re-evaluate your goals and begin raising the bar. You will need to balance long-term practice that sustains progress with identifying your next developmental focus or goals.

Altogether, this step invites you to be more conscious of actions as well as tangible barriers. Identify the elements in your life that support the continual realization of your goals. Also, examine the events and relationships that interfere with your vision and goals. It is critical to remove as many barriers as possible and to stop behaviors that no longer align with your development goals.

The overall objective in this chapter is to understand your habits and choices, and to confirm they are aligned with your long-term goals.

Tools

Below is a table you can use to capture and track your progress. For many people, the simple act of recording their progress in writing helps maintain their commitment. Use the following worksheet to help track your progress against each of your goals. If you would like to see a sample, review Joey's answers later in this chapter.

TABLE 8-1 PERSONAL TRANSFORMATION ACTIVITY/PRACTICE LOG TEMPLATE							
Goal	Action	Record Actual Performance	Expected Impact	Priority	Measure	Progress	Feedback from Whom
Top 1	1.						
	2.						
	3.						
Top 2	4.						
	5.						
	6.						
Top 3	7.						
	8.						
	9.						

Joey's Development Journey Continued

Joey will now walk through her worksheets and journal entries for embedding change systematically.

PERSONAL TRANSFORMATION ACTIVITY/PRACTICE LOG - JOEY'S EXAMPLE

Goal	Action	Record Actual Performance	Expected Impact	Priority	Measure	Progress	Feedback From Whom
Top 1	1. Meditate 10 min/day	Mon - 10 min Tues - none Wed - none Thurs - 5 min Friday - 20 min	Calming composure, emotional balance	1	Frequency of meeting goal	Met goal 3x this week	Spouse – impact of calm Colleague – impact of composure
	2. Don't react until I understand issue at hand	Mon - yes Tues - yes Wed - no Thurs - yes Friday - yes	Retain high morale	1	Staff morale	Daily	Management team Direct service staff
	3.						
Top 2	4.						
	5.						
	6.						
Top 3	7.						
	8.						
	9.						

Innovative Leadership Reflection Questions

To help you develop your action plan, it is time to further clarify your direction using reflection questions. Questions "What do I think/believe?" reflect your intentions. "What do I do?" questions reflect your actions. The questions "What do we believe?" reflect the culture of your organization (i.e., work, school, community), and "How do we do this?" questions reflect systems and processes for your organization. This exercise is an opportunity to practice innovative leadership by considering your vision for yourself and how it will play out in the context of your life. You will define your intentions, actions, culture, and systems in a systematic manner.

Table 8-2 contains an extensive list of questions to appeal to a broad range of readers. You will likely find a few of these questions fit your own personal situation; focus on the ones that seem most relevant. We recommend you answer one to three questions from each of the categories.

TABLE 8-2: QUESTIONS TO GUIDE THE LEADER AND ORGANIZATION

What do I think/ believe?

- How do I honor the progress I have made while maintaining focus on the balance of the work that needs to be done?
- How do I deal with both profound progress and a need for continued change?
- How do I deal with unresolved issues and uncertainty as I move forward?
- How do I deal with my desire to fix this issue and get back to the "real work?"
- What progress have I made as a leader/person?
- Are my assumptions still valid?
- As I have changed, am I still in the right role for my personal values and mission?
- How do I define myself as a leader? How do I think about my role and impact? How does my story about my effectiveness support or hinder my continued success?
- How does my belief about myself differ from how others see me?
- Am I still committed to the practices I developed?
- Am I willing to make these practices part of my life long-term?

What do I do?

- What do I communicate that conveys both progress and continued urgency?
- Am I visibly doing what I have committed to doing?
- Am I living up to the standards I have set for myself?
- Am I perceived as acting with integrity with regard to meeting my commitments?
- What do I do that reinforces the impact of my personal development?
- What do I do to sustain my new practices and development?
- How am I continuing to show the new behaviors I have publicly and privately committed to?
- How do I continue to sustain the practices I have started and the behavioral changes I have made? Have these changes become part of who I am, or will I slowly slide back to old behaviors—especially under stress or as other priorities emerge?
- Do I surround myself with others who are focused on their personal changes so that I have a reinforcement system?
- Do I continue to track and measure my progress?

What do we believe?

- What do we believe about people who are always focused on their development?
- What do we believe about ongoing development practices vs. fixing problems then moving on?
- What do we believe about how to monitor and build momentum in different areas of life?
- What do we believe about appropriate pace and focus on development and growth?
- How do our beliefs about growth impact our ability to maintain momentum?

- What recognition is appropriate from different groups in my life (family, work, etc.)?

- How do we see ourselves now? How has our image of ourselves changed based on my personal change?

- Will the organization's goals and values change based on my personal changes?

- How do we react to old behaviors that no longer support the organization?

- If our organizational stories about who we are change, do we incorporate new jargon, best practices, and human interest into emerging organizational stories?

How do we do this?

- What are the top three new behaviors others can expect to see? How will these behaviors be measured and reinforced?

- Who will remind me when I am struggling that I can make these changes?

- Do I clearly understand how my personal changes impact my work? Have I started to change the way I do my job? Have I informed others (discussed with others) how their jobs or tasks will change based on my changes? If my changes impact how we interact, have we agreed on the new way we will work together? Are we following a structured plan to perform consistently according to a new structure or guidelines?

- Do we need training to support new behaviors or interactions?

- What happens if I am not successful in meeting my top three goals? How would I like others to reinforce and/or support my behavioral changes?

- Do we have systems in place that discourage me from successfully accomplishing my top three goals?

- What processes/measures will we establish to identify behaviors that are no longer appropriate or necessary? What can I stop doing that will give me more time to practice?

- Are there any new ways to gain additional momentum to leverage existing changes and/or small wins?

- Am I reviewing measures regularly and recognizing results toward my change goals?

- Does the organization acknowledge leaders who have made the desired changes (job starts and stops) and mastered new skills? Am I being rewarded for my personal development in this system?

- Do we continue to measure and reward actions that are necessary to sustain the changes using the updated job descriptions and process metrics? Am I still a good fit within this system?

- Has the organization rewarded me with recognition, promotion, increased responsibilities, or financial rewards?

- Will others be expected to demonstrate behaviors and skills that I developed during my change? How will their changed behavior reinforce my new skills and behaviors?

- Have we sufficiently updated employee orientations and other human resources, and IT systems to support changes in goals and values for our leaders?

- Are we reviewing objective and subjective measures regularly and recognizing desired leadership behaviors for me and others?

- Are we reinforcing actions that positively influence the larger vision while inquiring into those that do not?

- Have we developed and tracked success?

Joey's Reflection Question Responses

We will now walk through Joey's answers to one or two questions from each section of Table 8-2. Simply follow along with Joey to answer the questions for yourself, or select the questions that fit your current situation.

What do I think/believe?

- *How do I honor the progress I have made while maintaining focus on the balance of the work that needs to be done?*

  In some areas my progress encourages me to go forward, while in others, the changes I am making scare me, causing me to experience a sense of regression. Still, I am making progress in my ability to take additional perspectives and becoming more adept at looking at my competing commitments. In some ways, I am really excited about these new insights, and am also excited about letting go of old fears and old behaviors. I feel relieved. As I say this, I also realize much of my behavior is based on old habits. I need to be very attentive to avoid making decisions out of habit or fear.

  I believe that I will continue to focus on my own growth while trying to balance my life. The level of focus will ebb and flow based on other life events and circumstances, and I am becoming comfortable with that. I trust that I will continue this path because I hold my own growth as a core belief about who I am and how I live my life.

- *What progress have I made as a leader/person? Are my assumptions still valid?*

  I believe I have made significant progress toward becoming more conscious of my behaviors and practices and how they impact my intentions. I have also made great progress in balancing my life. As I make these changes, I see that my assumptions are still valid and that my direction is still appropriate for me. With the dynamic steering approach, I believe I have the freedom to change my daily course of action while maintaining my overall direction.

  I am committed to turning the actions in my plan into ongoing life practices. I can see that I am much more effective as a person and as a leader when I make time to care for myself, by including sleep, diet, exercise, and meditation in my life. I am also more compassionate and easier to work with when I take the time to consider problems and opportunities from many different perspectives, including the perspective of the person I may think is causing me the problem.

What do I do?

■ *What do I communicate that conveys both progress and continued urgency?*

Probably the best way for me to communicate my urgency is through my actions. I actively participate in a personal development practice. I communicate this practice and ask for feedback. My main sources of professional feedback are my employees. We work very closely together, so they are able to provide a daily perspective.

Additionally, I continue to work with my support team and my coach, which has been really helpful. Each is able to offer insights, recommend practices, and help me maintain my focus.

■ *What do I do to sustain my new practices and development? How am I continuing to show the new behaviors I have publicly and privately committed to?*

I have found my personal reflection practice has turned into a regular habit. My colleagues are also using this practice, so it has become part of what we do. My meditation practice has always been important; however, now I find it even more important than I have in the past, as it allows me to stay centered and feel competent as the business grows and changes. On days when I am tired and do not feel like meditating, I remember that it is this practice that allows me to navigate life's difficult challenges with some level of grace and ease. I used to have my best ideas while in the shower, which was the only place my mind wasn't otherwise occupied; it amused me that I did some of my best thinking in the shower and I appreciated the ideas that flowed. I find I now create that empty space through meditation. The connection I make between the activity of meditation and the value it provides me on a daily basis keeps me committed even when I would rather do something else.

What do we believe?

■ *What do we believe about appropriate pace and focus on development and growth?*

The people in my newly revised organization place a significant emphasis on personal growth. This is one of the values of our culture. This means we ask for and provide feedback, and also make time to discuss development goals and strategies to support one another. While the agency does not overtly require participation in personal development initiatives, being around others who are heavily focused on self-development creates a subtle pressure to maintain individual advancements.

■ *What do we believe about ongoing development practices versus fixing problems then moving on?*

I have come to believe that ongoing developmental practices greatly reduce the need to fix problems. It allows us to continue to learn, to avoid potential issues, and to rely on and support each other's progress to meet our organization's goals.

How do we do this?

- *Does the organization acknowledge leaders who have made the desired changes (job starts and stops) and mastered new skills? Am I being rewarded for my personal development in this system?*

  Yes! I am being rewarded because the organization is thriving and I am impacting the world in ways I find important. I have a role within the organization that allows me to do the work I love to do and make a difference in my community and in the world. I also was honored by my peers with an award recently. While that's not why I do this work, it was a reminder that change, even change that is hard, is rewarded.

  We have also started to interview and select employees based on their fit into our culture. Since we all value physical and emotional health, as well as interacting with one another in a manner that respects differing points of view, we have created a rigorous interview process that selects candidates who possess these qualities and weeds out people who would not be supportive of these values. We believe that we will be more successful in our development at both personal and organizational levels if we surround ourselves with people who value similar things.

- *What are the top three new behaviors others can expect to see? How will these behaviors be measured and reinforced?*

  - Become more **conscious** of my behaviors and their impact on others, along with their alignment to my stated intention. Measure based on feedback from others and the absence of negativity or drama in my personal and professional life. Also note the absence of discussions where I am surprised about how I affected others (positively or negatively).

  - Feeling **calm and centered** in a way that will allow me to relate to others without distraction from wandering thoughts or emotions, increasing my ability to focus on the topic at hand. Measure based on my personal evaluation of how effectively I am performing and how often I feel distracted and unable to stay focused on the task at hand.

  - Ongoing **metrics** focused on growing the organization. These metrics are gauged by our increases in unrestricted income and attraction of high profile board members, reductions in small problems that, ignored or not addressed, could have become large problems, and increases in the number of children being served and the quality of that service.

Your Individual Process to Embed Innovation Systematically

Now that you have seen the worksheets and read through Joey's narratives, it is time to complete the worksheets and answer the questions for yourself. We encourage you to complete all of the exercises and answer one to three reflection questions from each section in Table 8-2. This process serves to help you clarify what your barriers to success are and how you will manage or remove them.

In summary, this chapter helped you create an action plan and conduct thought experiments needed to sustain the changes you have invested so much time to generate. At this time in history, we culturally reinforce the idea of lifestyle changes like diet and exercise. This is also true of leadership development, awareness, and skill building. To sustain the changes you have made and continue to build on them, it is important for you to continually approach them with deliberation and a sense of presence.

In our dynamic environment, growth and development are required just to stay relevant. This is perhaps more true now than at any other time in history, where growth is now a requirement to achieve and maintain success. Leadership growth is not only a matter of conceptual and pragmatic learning, but being introspective about our relationship with ourselves and others.

What do I think/believe?

What do I do?

What do we believe?

How do we do this?

How will you and your support team celebrate your success?

Conclusion

Congratulations! If you started with the first step, you have finished the innovative leadership development process, and we trust you have seen a significant increase in your professional and personal effectiveness. It is time to celebrate your successes and the support you received from others! How will you acknowledge what you have accomplished? Consider reviewing your vision and SWOT analysis, and write down what you accomplished.

How will you acknowledge the support others provided? How, in your culture, do you show gratitude and appreciation? When will you celebrate with your support team, either individually or collectively? Have you already been celebrating?

What Is Next For You?

Through this workbook, we provided a framework for developing innovative leadership to support your success. We augmented the process with a series of reflection questions and templates that can serve as guides. Based on our work with several hundred clients, we offer this specific combination of tools and framework to create a comprehensive approach that will allow you, the leader, to define what you want to change and give you a road map to support your development.

We also provided the story of Joey to illustrate how to use the development process from a nonprofit perspective. She uses the tools in the book and answers the questions to illustrate how a highly effective leader would engage in development. It is through Joey's explorations that we share the practical application of this theory with you.

Now that you have completed the workbook and established a solid personal development practice, it is time to think about whether you want to enhance your practice and begin the process again. Do you want to build on what you have created and revisit parts of the workbook that may be valuable at this time? You could start from the beginning and confirm your vision and values. Future iterations will likely take less time, as you now have experience with the development process. You may find that you focus in different areas based on your growth.

Congratulations on the progress you have made on your journey toward innovative leadership.

Enjoy your success!

Please note: Joey's experience is a composite of more than one person's experience, and examples of organizational challenges are a compilation. Any resemblance to specific situations or organizations is entirely coincidental.

Appendix

Board Process

To clarify how board meetings should be conducted and to ensure compliance with best practices, the following need votes:

- Mission and vision;
- Policies: personnel, crisis communication and management, finance, etc. Procedures do not need votes;
- Board meeting minutes;
- Financial reports;
- Agency annual budgets;
- Independent audits, including auditor's letters/qualified opinions;
- Plans: strategic, board development and resource development;
- Changes to the strategic direction of the organization;
- Hiring of the CEO;
- Campaigns;
- Opening, closing or changing signatures on bank accounts;
- Board members and officers being added or renewed.

Resignations are captured in the minutes, but do not require votes.

Board Member Criteria

While there are many constructs for boards, we submit the most effective board members will have:

- Commitment to attend meetings as well as do the work of the board
- Skills to move the organization toward its goals
- Disposable income to financially support the organization and encourage others to do so as well
- Passion to act as an ambassador for the organization and engage others in its mission
- Attitudinal fit to act in a manner consistent with the board culture and values

By-laws/Code of Regulation

The By-laws/Code of Regulations dictate the board's governance processes including size, meeting frequency, committee responsibilities, and structure which vary across agencies. Options include boards that meet monthly, every other month or quarterly; executive committees that make decisions or only recommendations between board meetings or that exist on paper but only meet in the case of a crisis; finance, audit, human resource, resource development, some variety of a board development committee and one or more program committees. Board size may range from three or 30 or more people.

Committees

Governance committees, which support the work of the board, are: executive, board development, finance, audit, resource development, and human resources as it pertains to policy or the CEO. In small and medium-size agencies, the finance committee often doubles as the audit committee, though that may become prohibited in the coming years.

Other committees that may meet will be ad hoc, created to respond to a specific time limited issue, or are operational in nature. Operational committees present something of a challenge to CEOs as they perform the work of the staff—which is the purview and responsibility of the CEO—but, the work is usually done by board members. In such cases, conversations about boundaries discussed in advance can prevent boundary creep. Operational committees work with staff to allocate resources and help determine the best use of those resources.

CEO and Chair Succession Planning

Because this book is focused on leadership, we focus particular attention on succession plans which put in place the process that will ensure leadership for an organization if the CEO or board president leaves abruptly.

In the case of the CEO, there is often someone who has been groomed for such an eventuality. Grooming may include being exposed to information and decisions outside the employee's normal scope of work in an effort to ensure the interim or long term success of the organization. If there is more than one person who has been groomed or is ready to ascend, care should be taken not to inadvertently provide access to confidential data, or imply that one person is favored over another during the search process. To avoid preferential treatment, or in an effort to share the responsibility, agencies that have a senior leadership team or a management team may have that team act as the CEO, making agency-wide decisions unanimously. When there is disagreement on the team the board chair or another board member can be the final arbiter. Another option is to contract with a consultant to provide that service. Some national agencies have a cadre of former CEOs who are available and/or a manager from an affiliate in neighboring city or county that may be a possibility.

In the case of the board president, a vice president who has agreed to become president provides the succession. It is helpful to avoid appointing a vice president who does not wish to serves as president and also to have identified a third person in line for succession if necessary.

Marketing Plans

Marketing plans are also widely used by nonprofits. Marketing, in nonprofit terms, provides opportunities for grand scale engagement and investment in an organization. Marketing plans include: policies, schedules, and assignments to ensure maximum and proper use of social media, speaker's bureaus, branding, design, web site, print and web media relations, newsletters and brochures drafting, printing and dissemination, and press releases, etc. Marketing plans define how and when your agencies will be presented to the community. It is important to discuss the goals of marketing. Is the organization marketing to donors, clients, or the community at large?

Please note that marketing is not fund-raising. Marketing raises awareness of the organization, while fund-raising raises money to support the organization.

References

Brown, Barrett. Conscious Leadership for Sustainability: How Leaders with Late-Stage Action Logic Design and Engage in Sustainability Initiatives. Ph.D. diss., Fielding Graduate University, 2011.

Collins, Jim. *Good to Great: Why some Companies Make the Leap… and Others Don't.* New York: HarperCollins Publishers, Inc. 2001.

Cook-Greuter, Susanne. *"A Detailed Description of Nine Action Logics in the Leadership Development Framework Adapted from Leadership Development Theory,"* www.cook-greuter.com, 2002.

Csikszentmihalyi, Mihaly. *Flow: The Psychology of Optimal Experience.* New York: Harper Perennial, 1990.

Fitch, Geoff, Venita Ramirez, and Terri O'Fallon. "Enacting Containers for Integral Transformative Development." Presented at Integral Theory Conference, July 2010.

Fritz, Robert. *Path of Least Resistance: Learning to Become the Creative Force in Your Own Life.* Toronto: Random House, 1984.

Gauthier, Alain. "Developing Generative Change Leaders Across Sectors: An Exploration of Integral Approaches," *Integral Leadership Review,* June 2008.

Goleman, Daniel. *Working with Emotional Intelligence.* New York: Bantam Books, 1998.

Goleman, Daniel, Richard E. Boyatzis, and Annie McKee, *Primal Leadership: Learning to Lead with Emotional Intelligence.* Boston: Harvard Business School Press, 2002.

Goleman, Daniel. *Emotional Intelligence.* New York: Bantam Books, 1995.

Heath, Chip and Dan Heath. *Switch: How to Change Things When Change Is Hard.* New York: Broadway Books, 2010.

Howe-Murphy, Roxanne. *Deep Coaching: Using the Enneagram as a Catalyst for Profound Change,* El Granada: Enneagram Press, 2007.

Johnson, Barry. *Polarity Management: Identifying and Managing Unsolvable Problems.* Amherst: HRD Press, 1992.

Kegan, Robert and Lisa Laskow Lahey. *How the Way We Talk Can Change the Way We Work: Seven Languages for Transformation.* San Francisco: Jossey-Bass, 2001.

Klatt, Maryanna, Janet Buckworth, and William B. Malarkey. "Effects of Low-Dose Mindfulness-Based Stress Reduction (MBSR-ld) on Working Adults." Health Education and Behavior. Vol. 36, no. 3. 2009: 601-614.

Leonard, George and Michael Murphy. *The Life We Were Given: A Long Term Program for Realizing Potential of Body, Mind, Heart and Soul.* New York: Tarcher/Putnam, 1995.

Maddi, Salvatore R. and Deborah M. Khoshaba. *Resilience at Work: How to Succeed No Matter What Life Throws at You.* New York: MJF Books, 2005.

Metcalf, Maureen. "Level 5 Leadership: Leadership that Transforms Organizations and Creates Sustainable Results." *Integral Leadership Review,* March 2008.

Metcalf, Maureen, John Forman, and Dena Paluck. "Implementing Sustainable Transformation – Theory and Application." *Integral Leadership Review,* June 2008.

Metcalf, Maureen and Dena Paluck. "The Story of Jill: How an Individual Leader Developed into a 'Level 5' Leader." *Integral Leadership Review,* June 2010.

Northouse, Peter G. *Leadership: Theory and Practice.* Thousand Oaks: Sage Publications, 2010.

O'Fallon, Terri, Venita Ramirez, Jesse McKay, and Kari Mays. "Collective Individualism: Experiments in Second Tier Community." Presented at Integral Theory Conference, August 2008.

O'Fallon, Terri. "The Collapse of the Wilber-Combs Matrix: The Interpenetration of the State and Structure Stages." Presented at Integral Theory Conference, July 2010 (1st place winner).

O'Fallon, Terri. "Integral Leadership Development: Overview of our Leadership Development Approach." www.pacificintegral.com, 2011.

Patterson, Kerry, Joseph Grenny, Ron McMillan, and Al Switzler. *Crucial Conversations: Tools for talking when stakes are high.* New York: McGraw-Hill, 2002.

Richmer, Hilke R. An Analysis of the Effects Of Enneagram-Based Leader Development On Self-Awareness: A Case Study at a Midwest Utility Company. Ph.D. diss., Spalding University, 2011.

Riso, Don Richard, and Russ Hudson. *The Wisdom of the Enneagram: The Complete Guide to Psychological and Spiritual Growth for the Nine Personality Types.* New York: Bantam, 1999.

Riso, Don Richard and Russ Hudson. *Personality Types: Using the Enneagram for Self-Discovery.* New York: Houghton Mifflin, 1996.

Rooke, David and William R. Torbert. "Seven Transformations of Leadership," *Harvard Business Review,* April 2005.

Rooke, David and William R. Torbert. "Organizational Transformation as a Function of CEOs' Developmental Stage." *Organization Development Journal* 16, 1, 1998: 11-28.

Senge, Peter, Art Kleiner, Charlotte Roberts, Richard Ross, and Bryan Smith. *The Fifth Discipline Fieldbook: Strategies and Tools for Building a Learning Organization.* New York: Doubleday, 1994.

Torbert, William R. *Action Inquiry: The Secret of Timely and Transforming Leadership.* San Francisco: Berrett-Koehler Publishing, Inc. 2004.

Wigglesworth, Cindy. "Why Spiritual Intelligence Is Essential to Mature Leadership," *Integral Leadership Review,* August 2006.

Wilber, Ken. "Introduction to Integral Theory and Practice: IOS Basic and AQAL Map." www.integralnaked.org.

Author Bios

Maureen Metcalf

Maureen is the founder and CEO of Metcalf & Associates, Inc., a management consulting and coaching firm dedicated to helping leaders, their management teams and organizations implement the innovative leadership practices necessary to thrive in a rapidly changing environment.

Maureen is an acclaimed thought leader who developed, tested, and implemented emerging models that dramatically improve leaders and organizations success in changing times. She works with leaders to develop innovative leadership capacity and with organizations to further develop innovative leadership qualities. Maureen is at the forefront of helping organizations to explore these emerging solutions for long-term organizational sustainability.

As a Senior Manager with two "Big Four" Management consulting firms for 12 years, Maureen managed and contributed to successful completion of a wide array of projects from strategy development and organizational design for start-up companies to large system change for well-established organizations. She has worked with a number of Fortune 100 clients delivering a wide range of significant business results such as: increased profitability, cycle time reduction, increased employee engagement and effectiveness, and improved quality.

Dani A. Robbins

Dani Robbins is the strategist, founder, and principal of Non Profit Evolution, a consulting firm dedicated to building capacity, including board governance and operational assistance, in nonprofit organizations.

Dani is an acclaimed thought leader, practitioner, and speaker, and has served for over 20 years in the nonprofit arena. Dani works with a variety of nonprofit boards and executive leaders to implement stronger and better-aligned organizations. When serving in executive leadership roles Dani turned around, reengaged, and created sustainability in two domestic violence shelters/rape crisis centers, two Boys & Girls Clubs and introduced the Women's Coalition—the prelude to the Women's Center—at Case Western Reserve University. She continues to work assisting organizations with board and resource development planning and training, strategic and tactical planning, senior leadership searches, and executive coaching.

Dani has a master's degree in public administration from the Levin College of Urban Affairs at Cleveland State University, a bachelor's degree from Kent State University, and is a graduate of Leadership Akron Class 22 and the University of Michigan's Ross School of Business/Boys & Girls Clubs of America's (BGCA) Advanced Leadership Program. She is the 2006 recipient of the Vision and Spirit Award from the Boys & Girls Clubs of America's Midwest Regional Office, and various organizations under her direction have been awarded multiple regional and national BGCA awards for diversity programming, web design, and media proficiency.

Dani is on the forefront of helping nonprofit organizations create goals, build systems to meet those goals, align their objectives, and thrive!

Thank you for reading!

Thank you for taking the time to read the Innovative Leadership Workbook for Nonprofit Executives. I trust the worksheets and reflection questions you completed here will help you become a more effective leader. Because growth has a ripple effect dynamic, we welcome your suggestions, additional tools and templates. Please contact me at:

Maureen Metcalf

Metcalf & Associates, Inc.

Maureen@metcalf-associates.com

This is the second in a series of workbooks. Subsequent workbooks will be written for emerging leaders, public service executives, and more. Download other titles on Innovative Leadership at www.innovativeleadershipfieldbook.com.

CPSIA information can be obtained
at www.ICGtesting.com
Printed in the USA
LVOW03s1150190116

471296LV00010B/49/P